Embrace Your Uniqueness

The Power of Being Different

Embrace Your Uniqueness

ReGina Norlinde

Author: ReGina Norlinde

Editing: Kathy DeSantis
         Anh Chi Pham

Cover Design: Katerina Dimova
              Gabriela Neyland

Norlinde ReGina, The Power of Being Different – Embrace your Uniqueness

ISBN: 978-0-615-25876-8

1st edition, September 2008

'If man would come to know the greater stranger – himself – let him enter his own closet and shut the door. There he will find his most dangerous enemy and there will he learn to master him. He will find his true self. There will he find the truest friends, his wisest teachers, his safest adviser – himself. There will he find the altar upon which God is the undying fire, the source of all goodness, all strengths, all power – himself."

(from "Life and teachings of the Masters of the far East" by Baird T. Spalding)

Acknowledgments

At times our own light goes out and is rekindled by a spark from another person.
Each of us has cause to think with deep gratitude of those who have lighted the flame within us.

- Albert Schweitzer -

My deepest gratitude to God and all my spirit friends and guides for helping me with all involved in writing this book. Thank you so very, very much for believing in me, guiding me through the process and helping me to feel safe to take action after receiving divine guidance.

A very special thank you to my mom for bringing me into the world, loving me and all the life lessons taught. My biggest hug to my sister, Baiba, and those in spirit world, my dear grandmother and my father.

A special thank you to my soul sister in Germany, Maya Hornbogen, for being the first one to accept me as I am. Thank you for being who you are as your example has helped me tremendously in trusting my power. Big hugs to Valerie and Sélina.

Many thanks to my dearest friend, Andrea Spielvogel, a true Earth Angel, who although thousands of miles away (in Scotland) is supporting me in every way possible. Thank you for being who you are and being there for me always and in all ways!

A special thank you to my pixie (no mischief here though) friend Jolene Johnston in California, for supporting me at all times, through my biggest challenges and greatest joy! I love you!

Thank you from the bottom of my heart to another Earth Angel, Kathy De Santis, for being her magnificent self and helping me produce my "masterpiece" – investing energy and time in editing. A special thank you to her furry assistants in her work!

Also thanks to my "down to Earth" Angel, Anh Chi Pham, for helping me with editing, for her time and energy added to this book.

Thanks to Katerina Dimova and Gabriela Neyland for their creativity in helping to design the cover for the book.

I extend my gratitude to all the great authors and teachers whose work has helped me on my life's journey, especially during times of changes (writing this book was a huge change in my life): Doreen Virtue Ph.D.,

Louise L. Hay, Colette Baron-Reid, Denise Linn, Steven Farmer Ph.D., Ester and Jerry Hicks.

Thank you to my miraculous angelic belly dancing friend and teacher, Jheri St. James, for being who you are and being in my life.

Finally my deepest thank you to all the yoga teachers whose classes I have been taking during the time of the birth of this book: Nora Mangiamele, Karta Singh, Erika Faith-Hattingh and Sotantar Salvador. Practicing yoga and being in your classes has greatly expanded my awareness, helped me to accept changes on deeper level than before and take the next steps in life with ease.

I love you all!

Blessed be.

ReGina

Table of Contents

INTRODUCTION

The Purpose of This Book

Each person comes into this world with a specific destiny--he has something to fulfill, some message has to be delivered, some work has to be completed. You are not here accidentally--you are here meaningfully. There is a purpose behind you. The whole intends to do something through you.

- Osho -

This book was born through Divine Guidance and therefore I trust you are reading it because you have followed your Divine Guidance to do so.

Now that the Law of Attraction is becoming well known and practiced globally, it appears that humanity is expanding to a new belief system that unlike before, is based in our heart, our passion, our feeling and love.

During times of changes of any kind the question of "Who am I?" is brought to our awareness on a deeper level than ever before. One way or another, eventually inventory of our life is required to better understand different parts of it or altogether.

When we repeat thoughts and behaviors that cause uncomfortable situations it is because we are in our comfort zone. As long as no changes are made, everything stays the same. When changes happen, no matter where in our life we are, we are "asked" to look for different ways of being. Ideally, when we make changes we want them to be for the better. In order for them to lead us to a better life it's important for us to know ourselves on the soul level. Knowing ourselves leads us to recognizing our uniqueness, accepting ourselves for who we are and realizing the strengths of who we are, the power of being different.

In my own life I have gone through the different stages in the process of embracing my uniqueness to reach the point where I can affirm: "I love my unique self and I am proud to be different!" and mean it My belief is that all of us deserve to be in touch with our true self as this is what leads us to live the life of our dreams. I came to this conclusion because of my own experience.

As you will read in later chapters in this book, all my life I had felt like I was expected to be someone else, act differently than I was, be, walk and talk differently. For a long time, that is what I was trying to do – please others even when I didn't know what exactly was expected from me. I would focus only on what others wanted, imagining what others would want instead of what I wanted or who I truly was.

Also, even when I was trying to do and be like everyone else, it didn't work, I didn't feel accepted, and I would get myself into embarrassing situations. It seemed like no matter how hard I was trying to please others and fit in none of it made my heart sing. I had this feeling that I needed to act like someone else in order to be loved and accepted.

So there I was sadly going through my life feeling that something was not quite right, but not consciously aware of what it was. There was nobody to talk to about it, nobody to help me see things from a different perspective, encourage me to be who I am and let me know that I am loved just the way I am.

At times I got very frustrated looking at people who seemed to fit in, seemed to have an easy time to be part of a group as that's when I felt like something was wrong with me.

It was quite a journey for me to come to the point where I am today – loving myself and knowing that I am loved for who I am, knowing that it is safe to be who I am and knowing that there is a whole world out there that has been feeling like I was which meant, as I learned there was and is nothing wrong with me nor with anyone else who feels this way.

My journey has been filled with different emotions, feelings and situations, I have met many wonderful people who provided me great lessons. It wasn't like one day I woke up and decided that I was going to be who I am. It was a process combination of different circumstances in my life, people I met, situations created, books read, spiritual teachers I met, workshops and classes taken, teachings heard, my experience in the past, tears and fun times, knowledge gained on all levels of my being, intuition and messages received from Spirit (God, angels, fairies, dragons…), knowingness that came from connecting with my inner voice, lessons learned through challenging situations, experience gained through conducting spiritual teaching and taking inventory along the way.

A major "topic" of my life's journey has always been: being different no matter where I go and working towards being happy with being different, being my unique self.

I have always wanted to make the world a better place and help people enjoy their life to the fullest. I found that we can do it only if we have learned to enjoy ourselves to the fullest. In this book I want to share my journey in hopes that it helps you in your journey.

Having gone through the process of learning the value of being different, experiencing the benefits of being who I am, my highest intention with this book is to help everyone accept and embrace their uniqueness and experience the power of being who they are, realize that it's okay to be who they are, it makes life much lighter and more fulfilling on a soul level.

This book offers you a way to explore your true self through stories and exercises. My hope is that it awakens different aspects of your true self and leads you to recognize and experience the power of your uniqueness as well as embrace it.

I want you to feel safe and empowered to be your true self no matter what happens and live the life of your dreams that we all so richly deserve.

Since my belief is that the most powerful learning and teaching happens through our own experience, this book is divided into two parts.

Part I is autobiographical therefore dedicated to true stories that were chosen to show the process I underwent to eventually embrace my power of being different and my uniqueness. Since I believe that all of our experiences help us not only understand our own situations better but also life in general, I trust that learning about our experiences helps others to see more clearly situations in their own life. My hope is that reading my stories will take you somewhere significant in your life.

Part II explores insights gained, lessons learned, messages channeled, exercises and meditations to help you to embrace your own uniqueness and power of being different. This part of the book is interactive and guides you to explore yourself deeper. My belief is that the most powerful and positive things in life are simple only we often have made them more complicated than necessary. This is the reason why many ideas shared in this part of the book are easy to follow. I encourage you to keep an open mind and follow through the exercises even if they might seem too elementary to be of any help. Experience the beauty of simplicity for yourself!

My dearest wish for you is to take what resonates with you, what you feel drawn to and enjoy being who you are as there is no more real and beautiful place from which to live our life.

Keep in mind - we might be able to lie to others, but not to ourselves. I invite you to enjoy your true self and live your life with truth. Shine your light to the world.

Love and many blessings from my heart to yours,
ReGina Norlinde

LATVIA

(Song Festival)

To better understand my journey of embracing my uniqueness, here are some facts and information about the situation in Latvia at the time I grew up. It gives a better sense of the challenges I had to overcome (not only me but everyone living in similar places and energies), beliefs learned and experienced. This explanation of my background will lend more clarity to my story and make it easier to relate and get the bigger picture.

I was born and grew up in Latvia – a country that is situated in north-eastern Europe with a coastline along the Baltic Sea in the middle of the two of the Baltic countries: Lithuania and Estonia, and across the sea from Sweden. There are about 2.5 million people living in Latvia and you can cross the country from one furthest end to another in about 5 hours by car (as you can imagine – quite small).

Latvia has four seasons and temperature can be as low as   -30 Celsius and as high as +30 Celsius.

A typical Latvian landscape is a mosaic of vast forests alternating with fields, farmsteads, and pastures; amid arable land are birch groves and wooded clusters, which afford a habitat for numerous plants and animals. In state forests (about half of all forests) and private forests, you may walk freely, pick berries or mushrooms; these forests are accessible by regular highways or country roads.

Latvia is among the few countries left in the world where natural ecosystems, largely untouched by man, still thrive in half of its territory.

It is a heaven for all those who seek to experience a land where nature and tradition have coexisted in harmony from time immemorial.

The soul of Latvia is revealed in the typical rural farmyard, where people live in harmony with nature's laws and rhythms. It is a place where ancient traditions are respected and annual festivals are joyously celebrated.

The Latvian landscape is also unimaginable without old trees. Oaks that are several hundred years old can be found in farmyards, as well as in the fields. Latvia also has become home to 9,000 - 10,000 pairs of white storks.

The Latvian language belongs to the Baltic group of the Indo-European family of languages. The first written texts in Latvian appeared more than 400 years ago, and since then the Latvian spelling has become one of the most perfect Latin script-based spelling systems in the world. Since from the Middle Ages till early 20th century the German language was the dominant language in education, science and administration. About 3000 German words have become part of Latvian vocabulary as well as English during the last decades.

Throughout history Latvia has been an independent country, but it was taken over by others (Germans, Russians...) and then regained independence.

Under Communist Rule

Half of my life I lived in Latvia when it was under Communist rule of the Soviet Union - a system of social organization in which property was held in common, a system, which allowed extremely little, if any, freedom of choice and uniqueness, a system where people were forced to follow the rules, speak and act as they were expected. It was based only on fear and rule breakers were more likely to get into major trouble (including their whole family). Being part of the former Soviet Union, Latvians struggled with the contradictory requirements of the Soviet regime.

Things have changed a lot since then and since 1991 Latvia is an Independent Democratic Republic.

Folklore

(Latvian Folk Group)

Because Latvians were denied the opportunity of developing a national, professional culture until the end of the 19th century, they expressed their creativity very powerfully in folklore. As a result there are over 2.8 million units of folklore material in the Latvian Folklore Archives, including over a million folk song texts and almost 30,000 melodies. In many European countries these ancient folk music traditions have practically vanished from social life. In Latvia, on the other hand, many ethnographic ensembles and folklore groups have inherited these ancient singing traditions directly from folk singers, or learned from descriptions notated in the relatively recent past. *Baltica*, the largest international folklore festival in the Baltic region is regularly held every year in one of the Baltic States - Lithuania, Latvia and Estonia.

(Dance Festival)

The festival *Kokļu dienas* allows those, who play the *kokle* - a traditional Latvian string instrument, to gather together and show their art. There is also an international folk dance festival *Sudmaliņas*, organized every other year. The aim of the dance festival is to preserve and popularize traditional Latvian dancing and to get to know dances of other nations, as well as to stimulate the development of new work based on folklore.

Latvian Song Festivals are well attended with a nationwide organization and annual festival program.

(Song Festival)

Every festival includes choir concerts and a street procession. The participants always wear colorful traditional costumes, the women with meadow flowers in their hands, the men with garlands of oak leaves. After the official conclusion of the festival, the singing continues almost the whole night through - in lodgings shared by the participants, in the open air, on buses and trains. For Latvians song festivals are not just festivals for singing, not just concerts with opportunities to show themselves and to view others, they are a symbol of national unity and identity. national rituals that are awaited with love, prepared for with respect, executed with full commitment and performed with honor. In this way they are analogous to the ancient seasonal rituals that marked the mythical cycle of time.

(Open-Air Museum)

Latvia's 3,000 year old cultural traditions are still a vital part of Latvian life today. The Midsummer solstice celebration of 'Jani' is just one of many holidays that continues to enrich the social lives of contemporary Latvians. Musical festivals, craft fairs and historical re-enactments attract the young and the old from all walks of life, and provide a look at values and traditions that have disappeared in many other parts of the world. In Latvia, traditions are not just a tourist attraction - they are a part of everyday life.

Discovering the Power of Being Different

"If you have anything really valuable to contribute to the world it will come through the expression of your own personality, that single spark of divinity that sets you off and makes you different from every other living creature."
- Bruce Barton -

Life consists of constant choices. You may have heard the idea that children choose their parents before they are born. In my life and work I have had plenty of experience and proof that this idea is true.

In the reality I live and know to be true every living soul has a choice, even on a soul level there is the choice to be born in a human form.

Just as we feel drawn to do certain things during our life here on Earth, to meet certain people, our soul feels drawn to be born in a physical body. The next step for a soul is to know exactly what lessons it wants to learn and experience while being here: it can be something completely new to the soul, it can be something soul has experienced already before, but wants to gain deeper understanding and knowledge. Then we as souls choose other souls to help us on our journey, we are chosen to be the teachers on someone else's journey. The more lessons we have chosen to learn and experience with each other, the better the chances are that we will be in each other's life during this life time for a long time. Once we have found and chosen the perfect match for our experience on Earth, we are ready to be born. Since family is who we usually spend the most time with – every family member has the greatest lessons to learn from each other and to teach each other.

On the soul level we all know that the source of "all that there is" is love and we choose other souls to help us on our journey, choose to help them on their journey because we love each other and honor the light within every living being equally as our own.

On the physical level this might be the judgmental world, but on the Soul level, once we look beyond the physical plane, there is no such thing as judgments as everyone and everything is honored as equal in all aspects. Everyone has his/her own purpose, everyone has his/her own mission, without one wouldn't be another and everyone knows it: just like without man and woman coming together to build a family there wouldn't be children, without each one of us being here on this planet, Earth would be uninhabited by humans.

Why have so many of us forgotten about this oneness and seeing each other as a unique and equal being of light? Our soul is endless, it doesn't have beginning or end, it doesn't have a form as long as it stays on the "soul plane" but once it's born in a physical body, the Soul suddenly is given a form and it's quite a tiny one, when we see a newborn's physical body. No wonder babies usually cry at birth – it can be quite a shock to " squeeze" the enormous soul into a tiny body, we might feel like we have been trapped.

Once we are born in human body, our journey of experiences and lessons start on the earthly plane. On the Soul level we do remember our purpose in life, we do know what we are meant to do, but often we are not conscious of it in our mind.

There is more to being a human than being a Soul. Being human is bringing heaven to Earth where heaven is our Soul and Earth is our physical body, and finding the balance between both. Often as we grow older we forget about this connection and our soul's purpose until some life changing event occurs (and it's different for everyone) and gives us a glimpse into something we already know, and then we spend the rest of our life remembering who we are and what we came here to do.

It really depends on the lessons and experiences we chose to learn and experience. In the past many souls have felt so trapped and restricted by being in a human body that they have decided to create even more restrictions and rules as the way of helping them to adjust to the life here with their inner feelings (often without having conscious awareness about it). As babies we start out with very little ability to do anything more with our physical body than sleep, eat when being fed, and pee/poop, we can move our arms and legs, smile and cry, and that's about it. Where as souls we know that we can do anything. Then, as we grow older, more or less we hear from parents or our guardians – don't touch it, don't go there, not that, no no no... more restrictions when all we want to do is try out new things. Please get me right – I am not saying that it's ok to let do children whatever they want, but if we look at these experiences from this different perspective, we can choose to add more positive energy and understanding when we need to use these restrictions.

As we grow we get restrictions on what to wear, how to have our hair done, what to say and many others. The truth is that most of the time these restrictions we give to our children (or the need we have to have pass on these restrictions) we have adapted from others, possibly even from our parents and family. We have been taught to listen to grownups because they know better, they know more, they know what's the best for children but is that always the real truth? What if children actually have greater knowledge and wisdom than the grownups believe they have? We can only be who we are and share the experience and knowledge we have, we can pass on beliefs that we have, but our reality and beliefs are most certainly not the only real and true ones. If we believe they are, it is one of the ways in which we can "help" a child's soul to feel even more trapped than it already might feel.

Once we grow up with different restrictions and learn more and more of them, they become part of our life and part of what's considered "normal", considered to be "standard". The more we adapt to this "normal and standard" way of life, we move away from our uniqueness, the connection between our Soul self and physical self becomes weaker and weaker. Often it might even lead to shutting down the spiritual part of ourselves. Divine spark within us can never be turned off and so depending on our choices in this life, sooner or later this spark reminds us of our truth, of our true self, of our mission. The first glimpse in remembering who we are often starts through some dramatic and even traumatic experience as many of us have this need to have something extreme happen only then we seem to notice things for what they are; car crash, serious disease, losing a loved one, strong spiritual experience, vision, dream coming true...

When awakening happens, many past and present experiences start to make sense, we begin to remember who we are and what we came here to do, we start to go with a flow, start to embrace our gifts and instead of following the crowd, we stand our ground and step by step reclaim our freedom.

Being in a physical body and feeling the freedom on a soul level requires us to get fully in touch of who we are, to get in touch with our true self and embrace our uniqueness. That's when we remember and rediscover the power of being who we are, the power of being unique, the power of being different again.

May the most significant experiences and stories from my journey that I share in following chapters help you to remember and become aware of your most significant life's stories. May they serve as an encouragement to look deeper within and become more aware of who you are. May the knowledge, wisdom and tools I have gained on my journey help you in yours. May it help you to get in touch with your truth and your true self, empower you to be who you are, remember and believe that anything is possible!

CHAPTER I

My Family's Role in My Journey

In every conceivable manner, the family is link to our past, bridge to our future.
- Alex Haley -

(our house)

It was another day at home in "Weshi" village - sunny and bright as most of the summer days are. It was such a great feeling to wake up with bird songs and fresh air coming in through the open window.

Fresh air blew my hair as soon as I walked outside, of course – we lived in a place that very easily could be considered "nowhere". Even though there was a main road in front of our house, cars passed by very rarely – and lack of cars was compensated with a great amount of trees all around the house, birds singing non-stop, deer and other wild animals visiting, especially during the cold winter months. We had a huge garden with different types of apple, currant and black-currant, and hazelnut trees, a vegetable garden with any vegetable you could think of, strawberries, lots of flowers all around the house that were beautifully growing and glowing from early spring till late fall. Wild flowers were seen abundantly around the house almost all year long.

We had a few huge, centuries old maple trees in front of the house and it was amazing to see squirrels play in these trees. In combination with other wild animals that visited us, all the cats we had, chickens and cows – it was almost like living in a real "Cinderella" story – and communicating with animals was as common as eating and drinking.

My Earth Angel Grandmother

Grandma always made you feel she had been waiting to see just you all day and now the day was complete.
                                        - Marcy DeMaree -

Everyone is special in their own unique way and when it comes to family members we often feel like they are the most special ones ever, which is so great. My grandma was one of those special people to me however she also seemed to be different from other people her age that I came in contact with. I didn't really know how exactly to put it in words, but I saw it and felt it. She didn't gossip like local women and just minded her own business.

We had this special ritual every morning: We would look through song books and my grandma would play songs on the piano and we would sing together. There was something special about this time together and I could just feel it.

(me at the age 4)

She was around 5'4 in height, slim, had clear blue eyes and hands that reflected the hard work. She always wore a dress.

(my grandma)

My grandma always seemed to be glowing and wisdom poured out of her continuously. Even as a child I felt like she was to be treasured, not only because of the fact that she was my grandma, but there was something more to it. She had this angelic energy: always in peace and always knowing what to do, very sensitive, especially to harsh energies around, all she ever wanted was peace. Looking back it sometimes makes me feel embarrassed and guilty, like I didn't appreciate her as much as I could while she was still with us.

We spent a lot of time together, even if we were each doing our own thing, very often it was just me and her home – so we shared a lot. One of the great passions that my grandma had was gardening. Whatever she touched in the garden grew vibrantly. She had a calendar that showed the right time to plant any seeds and work in the garden. One of the things she taught me to never plant seeds of vegetables that can have worms on a day that has "r" in it's name (like Thursday, Friday... but Tuesday for instance). It sounds weird but it worked! I didn't believe it so we did an experiment, planting seeds – in days with "r" and days without "r" and it was amazing to see how ones planted in "r" days were very much loved by worms, but the others grew healthy and were left un-touched. I was able to witness that these vegetables and fruits seemed to possess an invisible protective shield against worms and other plant-munching bugs.

The most important thing that my grandma always wanted, as I mentioned before, was "peace". She kept saying that the greatest gift to her would be all her family being in peace, living in peace. I didn't quite understand what exactly she meant by that, when I was little. Perhaps because there was quite a lot of arguing going on in our house and I was quite "talented" in "destroying" the peace at home. I associated the word peace as a synonym to mean "no-war". Since in our country was long gone and peace was already there, I dismissed my grandma's words. Of course the older I grew the more I came to understand the greater meaning of peace, which I describe later in this book.

I really loved my grandma. She was actually the only one I truly cared for. I did know how to show her my feelings. In my family it wasn't a common thing to hug each other and say "I love you". I did picture myself coming inside and giving my grandma a big hug, but when it came to actually doing it – I would freeze. She knew that I loved her anyway. She was like an Angel for me – always there, always caring. We had a bond and connection between us which seemed to grow with time.

Grandma had had quite a challenging life – she was happily married, had three wonderful kids, but while building the house we lived in now her husband (my grandpa) had an accident and passed away. Ever since that moment, all the household work was done by my grandma, including raising children, taking care of all the animals and the garden. Although now I realize her life was in perfect divine order it felt very unfair at the time. Even to me as I grew up without my grandpa. I was told many great and fascinating stories about him and would have loved to have him in my life.

Keeping the Promise

When I was about 14 years old and no longer lived at the same house with grandma we had a conversation with my grandma about getting older, passing over and death. My grandma was concerned that the time might come when she needed someone to be with her at all times. She didn't want to experience that and asked me to promise that if something like that ever happened, I would do whatever it took to help her pass over quickly. I was "freaked out" but I felt like the only thing I could do was to promise her to take care of her request.

This is when I miraculously discovered the connection between our world and spirit world. That night before falling asleep I asked for some guidance to help my grandma to stay healthy. I also asked that whenever the time comes for my grandma to pass over, it happens quickly, easily and naturally. I suddenly saw my grandma in my mind surrounded by white light with bright light beaming out of her and bright light all around her. I heard someone telling me to repeat this affirmation: "my grandma is healthy, she lives a long and healthy life and all is well." It was so strong that I couldn't avoid hearing the words and seeing the vision. Since it came like the answer to my question and concerns, I went with it.

From that moment on every single night just before going to sleep, I did the visualization and affirmations to help my grandma stay healthy just the way she wanted to be.

Many years later as I started to study at the University, I was home only for a few days a month, I also was guided to feel the love I have for grandma in my heart and send it to her – heart to heart, which I did. We never ever spoke about our "deal" and promise again, but grandma sure was extremely healthy – at the age of 84 she didn't take any medicine (she didn't need to), didn't need to wear any kind of glasses to be able to see near or far, she had a great spirit and a sharp mind as if no age mattered and I was happy to see it.

33

One Sunday night as I left to go back to the University, I felt like something wasn't quite right, but since I couldn't pinpoint it, I just hoped all was well. While I was on the bus sleeping, I suddenly woke up with a feeling like I was stabbed in my heart, I checked the time and tried to relax but I couldn't fall asleep. About two days later, I received a letter from my mom asking me to call because my grandma was in the hospital. Mom said it was an emergency. What I found out was – my grandma had said: "I am dying!" and lost consciousness at exactly the same time I woke up in the bus. She was taken to the hospital and doctors said she might get better, but if she did someone would need to be with her all the time. My heart was pounding as I remembered the promise I made to my grandma and felt like this was the time when my grandma needed me but I couldn't even imagine myself asking someone to help her die.

I was extremely spaced out that day and night. I sat down for meditation without knowing how, but I knew I had to do something. I was seven hours by bus ride away from home. I had to do something before I went home. I decided to ask the Universe to help me. I told it in my mind the story and all my concerns, my grandma's wish and her situation as much as I knew, I asked for forgiveness about all the times I wasn't nice to my grandma, didn't listen to her. I was carried away by prayers and pouring my heart out to the Universe. From all my heart I asked that everything be arranged so that if my grandma is meant to live and she can be her healthy self without needing someone to be there 24/7 to help her to heal, if she was to live and have someone to take care of herself, which she didn't want to happen, to help her pass over. After I had said and asked all I could think of, I sat quietly for some time. Suddenly I felt such a relief run over and through me and I went back to sleep at a little bit past 4AM.

The next morning when I woke up, I felt lighter. When I called my mom I found out that grandma had felt better last night and then had passed away just a little bit past 4AM. Thank you God and the Universe! Even though I was sad, I was grateful to hear about what happened as I knew that's what my grandma wanted and it was for her highest good.

✦⸎🦋⸎✦

This was the time when I got interested in life after death. I read all the books that had any information about it. The idea that resonated with me was that for 40 days spirit stays close to earth as being in transitioning space, which I truly believed as I could feel my grandma with me all the time. Her name day (just as celebrated day in Latvia as birthday) was coming up and it fell just within the last end of 40 days. I had promised to sing my grandmother's favorite song as a gift to her, which I did and then I felt like she moved on. It was like she was waiting for me to sing to her, which I never did before.

The first year after her passing I could see her and other deceased family in my dreams, including my dad. All the relatives were so happy to see me and I was consciously aware during my dreams where I was. It was special and I felt very blessed for the experience.

I have reconnected with my grandma in spirit and we are having a great time talking to each other! I find it interesting that language doesn't matter when it comes to communicating to deceased loved ones: my grandma didn't speak English in this lifetime, but she sure speaks it now.

My Parents

Mother's love grows by giving.
- Charles Lamb -

"When I grow up I will never ever be like you, I don't want to be like you, nothing at all!" I remember always telling my mom. I always dreamed of having a mom like a friend I can talk to, who understands me, who loves me for who I am. My biggest dream was to have both a mom and a dad, as well as a sister and for all of us to be a happy, easygoing family. I wanted to be able to express myself and be heard. Most of all I wanted to feel loved and accepted.

I daydreamed and also had the most amazing dreams at night. I chose to be born in a family who was far from my ideal. I was the only child in the family and in our entire village. Mom was at work all day long and when she was home, all she wanted to do was sleep.

When it came to my dad – I knew I had one, but I never knew him. In fact, he was never mentioned in my family. My mom became extremely angry at me whenever I asked about dad so I learned pretty quick if I wanted to avoid her anger, I better not ask about him. All I had were dreams about my dad and I sure let my imagination flow to make up for not having other kids to play with. I taught myself to read at the age of 4 and had read just about every single children's book at home and in the local library. My favorite story was about twin girls who met each other in summer camp for the first time, and after finding out that they are sisters, they switched places. The story had such a happy ending and I could so relate as I was reading; The twin's mom never spoke about their dad, and the dad never spoke about their mom. After reading the book "Parent trap" I imagined I had a twin sister somewhere. I loved to think about my dad that way as well and that I would meet both of them one day in a real life. Just the thought made my heart sing. So I spent days having my pretend sister as an imaginary friend, and also talking to my dad. Soon I learned that not only my imaginary sister joined me in my games, other spirit beings came that I couldn't identify, I just knew they were there.

My mom was full of anger and frustration, full of negative thoughts and expectations. Most of the time I saw her, she was doing one of two things – either being angry about something or someone (including me), or sleeping or talking about needing to sleep. We did have some fun together once in a while but mom was completely opposite in personality to grandma.

I felt so much despair over my mom that I often wanted to die. My thinking was that then mom would notice me and finally appreciate me. I even ran away from home, however I ended up coming back several hours later. I felt my grandmother's pain and sadness seeing us argue which was the only reason I decided to come back and deal with mom.

When I started to go to kindergarten and primary school, I soon realized that I was not like the other kids. I couldn't really tell what made me so different, but I seemed to have the hardest time making friends or being part of a group. I tried my best to be likeable, but it didn't help. It got worse when other kids at school started making fun of me. One of the things they teased me about was the fact that I didn't know anything about my dad. I was the only one in the whole class who lived with a single mom. I was told that I was probably adopted and that my mom was such a bad woman there was no way I would be any different. That made me extremely upset – for one I didn't have anyone to talk to about it and the other problem was – I really missed having a dad and was already upset with my mom for not telling me anything about him.

I remember there was this song that I really loved on one of our old records we had at home. One day my mom came home as I was listening to it and completely lost control of herself. She turned the player off, yelled at me to never ever listen to this music again and accused me of giving her a hard time. I had no idea what she was screaming about, but I was in tears. I cried into my pillow until it was almost soaking wet. This hurt me a lot and again I wished I was dead. I felt like everything I did was completely wrong, I didn't know how to be. I felt over and over that I was expected to be someone I was not. I kept trying to guess what the expectations were, but I was wrong and I felt like I was from somewhere far away and I wanted to go back home. I wanted to be gone into my dream world where things were happy and in peace. I didn't have the slightest feeling of belonging. I couldn't relate to my mom in anything. We were so different! I was happy to be different than she was. I couldn't remember any real and truly happy thing that we ever did together as all was covered with anger, resentment and fear. My mom was also extremely afraid of what other people might think of her. It was the same about my dad too. She didn't want to tell me anything about him because she was afraid I would tell others in school. I had no choice but stay with the unknown and my dreams.

My dad was "involved" in her great anger with the record player. She told me later that the song I loved so much was my dad's favorite song and she couldn't bear to hear it. I believe that was the first time I felt a true connection with my dad. I knew how unfair it was for my mom to get mad at me, when her anger was because of the way she felt inside. I was almost 20 years old when my mom finally dared to open up about my dad, who he was, and what happened.

He had died when I was a baby, so the feeling that I had of his presence around me was validated.

On a positive note, my mom has been such a giver all her life, often giving more than she was ready to receive back. I don't really think she knew how to allow herself to receive. She believed that she wasn't worth anything, that she wasn't worthy or deserving. She would make sure others felt good, but not her. I got angry with her many times for this reason. I think she did a lot of that to compensate for her guilty feelings.

Also, I have always loved the way how my mom has creatively given life to many things like my stuffed bear that has pants on with a little pocket in front. As a kid I would often find some candy, messages or stickers in it which I loved. My mom could create something nice from nothing for a gift. For instance, a new birthday card from old cards.

(my mom & me)

While I was traveling she would send me some dried flowers from our home. When I lived in Scotland, my Christmas wish was to have some Latvian gingerbread cookies (they are so yummy). Apparently post office regulations didn't allow cookies to be mailed – so my mom made a Christmas card with a gingerbread cookie as part of the card. I loved and still cherish these tiny, creative notes. Even now I have never heard my mom say that she loves me, I know she does and these little creative gifts make me feel the love coming from her heart.

...Modern psychology tells us that women unconsciously choose a husband who reminds them of their dad on some level. In a way this makes sense, in a way not. Keeping in mind this idea, I wondered how a relationship with my Mr. Right was going to turn out to be as I never had a father figure in my life.

I was really excited when my mom met my sister's father, but their relationship seemed so complicated. I really liked it when he talked about the spirit world which intrigued me. He used to tell me about other dimensions and worlds and that only a few people can see them. He would say this funny thing (at that time I thought it to be funny) where before he sat down he would say to those from other dimensions and world: "Move, move. Make space for me as I want to sit down here!" And then he would move his arms as if to push someone sitting there aside. Even though I didn't admit it at the time, I truly believed that he was right, that there were other worlds around us and spirits too.

I loved seeing my mom happy for once, unfortunately, soon I learned the "dark" side of her new friend when he came over to our house while my mom wasn't there. He seemed to know exactly when was I home by myself. I was 12-13 years old when I learned and experienced sexual abuse. I knew it wasn't right that he came over when mom wasn't home, the way he talked, the way he touched me, the way he kissed me. I was completely clueless with what was happening, I didn't know how to say it, but I knew it wasn't right. His visits became regular and more often, and finally I couldn't stand him anymore. I told my mom that I didn't want him at the house when she was not there, I told her that I didn't want him to touch me or to kiss me the way he did.

I had always had this funny feeling from my mom that I am was her way, that I was not to be taken seriously and that I was a curse to her. This feeling came back again. My mom was convinced that I misunderstood something and that her boyfriend couldn't possibly intend anything bad. If there was any trust between my mom and me at this point it was completely gone. "It's not fair!" was the only thought that came to my mind. My mom would not protect me and stand up for me once again. I knew she did her best with what she knew at the time, but that didn't help matters. I felt completely helpless. My whole world went upside down. I started to come home late, if "he" was in our home, I would sit outside in the dark so nobody would see me and wait until mom was home alone. I couldn't bear the idea of talking to him. My grades in school dropped from A's to B/C's. I would be on my own a lot as I felt I couldn't trust anyone. I was not loved by anyone, I was not worthy to be taken seriously. (My grandma didn't know anything about it all as my mom and I had moved to live in a city when I was 10 years old, and I didn't want to upset her). Deep down I knew this not to be true, but all my outside experiences were proof that it was true. I didn't know how to deal with life, how to be and I would catch myself dreaming about the best ways to kill myself again. As before, when I felt bad, I felt like my grandma was with me as an angel who was helping me to make wise choices and thanks to that I believe I am alive today.

Being away from home as I have been in recent years as well as working on my spiritual growth has helped me to release the anger and hate that I had towards my mom and what she did and did not do for me.

A few years ago I was shown in one of my past lives that my mom was my sister who had fallen in love with my boyfriend who I was about to marry. Her attempts to kill me with a knife were successful in this past life. I was also shown how this life was intended to be about her making up for killing me by being my mom – the one who gives me birth, a chance for both of us to make up for the past and smooth things out. I am grateful to be given this opportunity. I am grateful be alive at this time.

A Dream Coming True - My Sister

At the age of 14 a very happy thing occurred that made me feel much better about life - my dream about having a sister became real. I was so excited to learn a baby was on the way. I was certain it was going to be a sister, as I had known her already since early childhood. Even though I couldn't play with her like with someone my age, I loved her so much and I loved the fact that I had a sister. Older ladies were whispering as I walked with a stroller and I could hear them saying "so young and already with a baby". That didn't bother me – I loved my sister a lot. She was so special and having her in my life was the greatest thing that had ever happened. No wonder – she seemed to have lightened up the whole family including all the challenging situations.

In fact, my sister's dad and my mom split up shortly after my sister was born and our family became a complete "girl" world again.

(we have a lot of fun together)

(my sister & me – we both love singing)

***

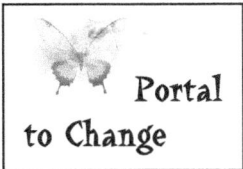

Portal to Change	*What are your most significant memories about your family and it's role in your life's journey?*

CHAPTER II

Early Spiritual Experiences

We change the world not by what we say or do, but as a consequence of what we have become.

- David R. Hawkins -

Early Signs

I walked out the door to go play outside. As soon as I closed the door behind me, I had the feeling someone was watching me. All I could think of was – RUN! I was running as fast as I could to get to the barn where my grandma was. Just before I opened the barn door to go in, I dared to look back in the direction, where I felt someone was watching me. Awwwwwwww – I screamed inside as loud as I could. It was her again – the black snake, black cobra.

It felt like a female and she had appeared almost every time I walked outside and sometimes even came inside. I was petrified, it was freaky weird and I wanted this to stop. I hoped that she didn't notice me looking and seeing her, but too late. I heard her "hissss" and in a flash she was over from across the street standing right in front of me. She didn't try to hurt me or do anything bad, it almost felt like she wanted to communicate, but I was too scared to allow the thought of making friends with her. Besides, what could a snake possibly have to say to me and what could we possibly have in common? I could only scream in her presence.

"Regina, Regina, are you all right?" asked my mom. Still not knowing what exactly happened, as I seemed to be somewhere else, not outside anymore, I slowly opened my eyes. My mom had turned the light on and I found myself lying down in a sweat. It was the middle of night, my screaming had woken up everyone in the house and my parents were concerned and worried. This was one of the many nights when I would have snake visits and my "friend" the black cobra visiting me during dreamtime, and I would wake up all scared and screaming... and, of course, waking up everyone in the house.

I wanted this to stop, but I had no idea what to do as it didn't feel like I had any control over it. I felt like snakes had taken over my dreams and sound sleep. I was scared every time I went outside as I had the feeling that snakes were going to attack me as soon as I showed up. If someone else was with me or if there were other people around but it didn't happen so often. I was the only child in the village and there was no other house nearby. I had a strange feeling about things being not quite right and whatever it was, it came from outside. I saw it in my mom's eyes, especially when things like snake visits at night happened to me. But at this point in my life, it was more than I could understand. I just knew there was something different and unusual happening, and I was part of it.

Little Witch

Ever since I could remember – I was drawn to all things magical. "**Little Witch**" by Otfried Preisler was my favorite book and I wanted to be a little witch so badly. It was my biggest dream – to be able to make magic happen to improve everyone's life. Little witch was only 127 years old and too young to party with the old witches. When she sneaked into a party and was caught, the old witches gave her an assignment to be a good witch for the whole year, then they might let her party with them. Little witch did her best to be good, she helped all who needed help. When the year passed, she went to see old witches, who were impressed with her ability to do spells, but when they found out all the good things little witch had dome throughout the year, they got furious. Turned out that by "good witch" old witches meant doing bad things to others, which wasn't what little witch was about. It ended with little witch being put to work as punishment to make a fire for the party. Little witch burned the old witch's brooms and spell books. So "good' won and I wanted to be a good little witch and make everything "good" win over "bad". I loved the idea of waving a magic wand or saying a spell and making it happen. So my daydreaming was filled with seeing myself as a little witch and imagining all the things I would "make happen" helping others and myself. Little did I know then that the essence of my dream and my dearest wish would become a reality in a different way than I ever thought.

(Herb Witch from "Latvian Mythology Card Deck)

Based on the ancient Latvian traditions - the idea and meaning of life, is to live in harmony with the cycles/rhythms of nature, other people, and oneself; in other words, to live well and thoughtfully. One of the most popular and well known Latvian folk verses says:

"Visi man labi bija,
kad es pati laba biju;
Visi mani naidenieki,
ja es naida cēlējiņa"

(Everyone is good to me if I am good myself; everyone is angry with me if I am the one anger comes from).

I didn't really understand the true meaning of this until I became consciously aware of spirituality. Then I also learned that what I knew to be "normal" growing up was known worldwide as paganism, the basis for witchcraft and people who practiced witchcraft were called witches. It was such a discovery for me that my wish to be a "little witch" was fulfilled just by me being born in Latvia.

If the ancient Latvians had been asked what their religion was, the meaning of the question would have baffled them. Their religion was their way-of-life.

The basis of Latvia's traditional folklore is verses, or *dainas*. The *dainas* are Latvians' main fountain of wisdom—the most useful wisdom and observations, tested by life and time. The Latvians have always lived in close association with nature, and nature was also a very important part of their ancient traditions. The whole world—from the smallest insect, grass seed and tiniest pebble, to the entire sea, stars and universe—is seen as a living organism and having God within by Latvian traditions. Latvians speak about and to God as with a friend. They often show special kindness and closeness to God by addressing him with the diminutive form.

Only those who do their best, no matter what it is, receive the best. The essence of God is believed to be wisdom and thought, original energy, Universe… Harmonious living is one of Latvia's ancestors' most fundamental insights; to be in harmony with nature, God, other people, and oneself.

In Latvian tradition every individual can choose his own interface with God. In the dualistic interpretation of God, Mâra is the symbol of the world of matter — she encompasses all of the material existence.

The third Latvian deity or aspect of God is Laima - decider of fate. She personifies that unbreakable law of the world, where each action has its consequence, similar to karma:

"Bēgu dienu, bēgu nakti,
Laimes likta neizbēgu,
Kādu mūžu Laime lika,
Tāds bij' man dzīvojot"

(I flee all day, I flee all night, but I cannot escape the fate set by Laima; I have to live the kind of life that Laima has given to me).

Laima gives everyone a certain kind of life, or fate, but one is still able to influence one's fate for the better or worse, depending on one's good or bad deeds and thoughts. To use one's mind and understanding, along with God's wisdom, to form and use the circumstances one has been given by Laima in order to fill one's life with good work and good deeds is then the "meaning" or responsibility of one's life.

Based on Latvian ancient traditions, Latvians believe a person consists of three parts: the physical body, the soul and the spirit. Often Latvians speak of This World where we are currently living, and the Other World or the world Behind the Sun where the spirit continues to live after physical bodies have died:

> "Šai saulē, šai zemē,
> viesiem vien padzīvoju;
> Viņa saule, viņa zeme,
> tā visam mūžiņam"

(I lived only as a guest in this sun, in this world; The other sun, the other world – that is forever).

Latvia's 3,000 year old cultural traditions are still a vital part of Latvian life today.

Our house was out in a nature and we lived our life following these rhythms. My grandma was a source of wisdom when it came to that. She always new what to do based on nature laws as well as she also used the folk verses in different situations in life.

The only drinks I knew growing up were natural juices and herbal tees. Herbs were a big part of my life growing up - my grandma always knew when was the best time to collect different herbs around our house. It was often my "job" to pick herbs. There would be different ways to dry them, what worked for some herbs didn't work for others. So we would have shelves filled with plain paper bags with herbs (those were the best to store herbs to keep all the goodness in). We picked our own berries, fruits and vegetables as well as harvesting honey. Just by looking at sky or tuning in, my grandma would be able to tell what the weather was going to be like.

If we got ill, we used natural medicine, even for cuts or bee stings. We always had all the necessary herbs and products in case there was a need for them, for example: raw potato for bee stings, aloe vera plant for any rash and itching or burns, chamomile tea was the best for anything, it was like universal herb – to drink as a tea, use it to calm upset stomach, use it to calm eyes… and the list continues.

As I said, I didn't know any different as I grew up, it was just the way it was.

Following this natural and magical note – nobody had ever told me, but I knew deep within that if I wanted something, I could make it happen. I also knew that, if something bad happened, some challenges appeared, somehow they would be resolved and afterwards I would feel better than ever before.

Most of the time, the sounds of nature were the only sounds that we would hear and I loved to listen to wind blowing, birds singing, loved watching clouds in a sky and see them play. 90% of the food we had was home made.

Oh well, I think you get the picture. After I started to travel and learned that similar ideas of living in "tune" with nature were basis for being a witch – my appreciation of my early childhood experiences became a million times stronger as I felt like my "being a little witch" dream had not only come true, but had already been true my whole life even if I wasn't aware of it.

(embracing my witchiness)

Lights and Orbs

Green, red, blue, yellow lights started to appear around the candles and lamps the longer I looked at them. It looked just like a rainbow and it was so beautiful. I could see rainbows everywhere, lights around the people and I discovered the more I looked the clearer lights became. I didn't know what exactly they were, but I knew that they were not really touchable in physical terms.

Sometimes they were clear, sometimes they looked a bit cloudy. I also discovered that even if I didn't see them with my physical eyes, I would know what color they were. It was fun to watch and I wanted to learn more so I mentioned it to my mom and grandma. They became very concerned when they heard about the lights and colors I saw. That's when I learned that not everyone sees them. My mom was convinced that something was wrong with my eyes and was ready to take me to the eye doctor. My eyes were well, but her reaction made me keep my experiences to myself which I did up until I started to study. That was when I picked up the book that had just come out "Aura's and How to Read Them". I was so excited to see pictures similar to what I was seeing and I was drawn into reading the book even more.

Luckily my friends accepted me and my "weirdness" for what it was and were happy to be the ones I experimented with. I discovered that I could see auras if I wanted to. The more I practiced the easier it became. I would sit in a class, look at the teachers and see colors around them. I also discovered that colors of aura changed depending on what the teacher was talking about and the feeling that was behind it. It was extremely exciting for me and I was very determined to dig deeper in this direction.

My discovery didn't stay secret for very long and it turned out that many of my classmates were interested in auras. Pretty soon I had people coming to our room to have me check out aura colors for them. I absolutely loved to look at auras and I felt like my life was beginning to have a whole new meaning.

Another exciting thing that I could see were orbs. I didn't really know what they were at first. I saw them as colored and moving lights that were fun to watch. I didn't really make any connection between when they appeared and how they moved. I was just fascinated by their presence and I knew they weren't going to do anything bad. I could feel peace from the orbs and a sense that they were watching over me.

Growing up, every time I heard the word "God", I had this image of an old man sitting on a cloud and watching Earth from above. It was what I had seen in books as our folk traditions had many folk songs and tales about God. I wasn't very convinced that this image I had represented the truth about God, but I knew one thing very clear – I was guarded by the Spirit Realm and the orbs were a clear confirmation of that. Whenever I went through great challenges I would get a feeling of knowing that all was taken care of and when I got through the challenges, I would feel much better than before them. Somehow I knew that everything would resolve in a mystical way.

On my radio show, I recently interviewed a guest who works with orbs and said that "Orbs are guardians of our Soul". As I heard it, something inside me "clicked" and then my earlier experiences made sense.

(in Laguna Beach, USA)   (in Scotland, UK)

Snakes

Ever since I could remember, I have had a snake phobia to the point where just seeing them on the picture would make me jump and throw the picture away. As I described before, I was often terrified to go outside as I felt like many snakes were waiting for me so they could attack me.

I continuously had dreams with snakes. The snakes that appeared were mostly cobras, once in a while some other ones were present. The snake I wrote about earlier was a special one as I kept seeing and feeling her presence strongly, when she was there, but she didn't always show up. I remember being surrounded by snakes as if I was a snake queen and it was terrifying for me. Endless nights waking up from fear of the experience – that was the way it continued until my adult years. In addition to my dreams, I saw snakes wherever I went. Nobody else seemed to notice them.

As I started to embrace my spirituality and healing power, snakes began to appear more than before. Now I had a different experience – there would still be my "favorite": cobras, but now they would swallow me, which to me seemed to be even more terrifying. Instead of seeing black majestic cobras, I would see a golden cobra with a crown on her head. I have to say the golden cobra was the snake that I felt like I didn't need to be afraid of which made me feel a little bit more at peace when seeing snakes.

Major changes happened when I made a connection with Atlantis for the first time through meditation. During this meditation, black cobra, the same that had been "haunting" me since childhood, was my best friend in Atlantis. I could feel the same energy as in my dreams and I was shown the same image of the snake across the road as I described earlier. Then I was shown the time when Atlantis fell apart and humans started to kill animals rather than staying friends. Afraid that I would kill her, the snake killed me first. All I remember from this experience was – shock, physical pain and relief. Then all went dark and it took me a while to get out of the meditative state. Like fast forwarding a movie, I saw a lot of scenes in my mind about snakes showing themselves one after another.

About a year later at a friend's home, I found out that her daughter had a corn snake as a pet. Even though I was scared at first, to my surprise I was able to get over it very quick. As my friend's daughter came near me holding her snake, my heart was pounding 10 times faster and I wasn't sure if I wanted to see the snake closer than 5 feet from me. But within a few minutes I had the snake in my hands and I was happy as I realized that my snake phobia was gone for good.

I have never been scared of snakes ever since and I wouldn't mind having a snake for a pet. I have also had many cobra visits in my dreams and meditations ever since and they have all been extremely healing. They put (energetically) some symbols in my hands, guiding me in doing energy work.

I have resolved my fear of these dreams with snakes and I am finally enjoying them.

Reflecting on my experiences with the invisible (except to me) snake I had, I decided to research what cobra, symbols, message snakes represent.

I learned that seeing snakes in dreams and during meditation can have different meaning. The most mentioned meaning of snakes says that they represent death and rebirth, a life changing transformation and new beginnings.

Article on an bellaonline.com says: "In Chinese astrology people born under the sign of the snake are considered extremely wise, sensual, and diplomatic--they have an ease of tongue which makes them able to navigate sticky situations. If a snake appears in your dream it may actually be there using its tongue to impart wisdom that may be life altering."

In the same article it says: "Snakes shed their skin which is a classic symbol for ridding oneself of what one no longer needs in favor of accepting that which is new. The process of shedding its skin is not simple for a snake, nor is it so in our waking lives. In nature, snakes become cranky, irritable, and are more likely to bite while shedding their skins. We often react in the same manner when releasing old, worn out lives and situations. We have grown comfortable with our 'skin' even if that skin has become a source of irritation. A snake appearing in your dream may very well be telling you that despite the temporary discomfort you must go through, it may be time to release old relationships, careers, or habits in order to renew and reclaim your life."

"When one is bitten by a snake in a dream, this often actually points to overcoming a situation that appeared dire. A snake bite dream may point to learning to overcome a situation and regain your power in life. Snake bites can be viewed as in injection of wisdom, rather than life threatening venom."

Few creatures evoke such strong reactions from people as snakes. People love them, hate them, or are downright phobic of them. Given the intense response snakes provoke, when one finds its way into your dream it is a good sign that the snake has something important to say about your life."

Dr. Steven Farmer in his book "Animal Spirit Guides" writes: "If cobra shows up, it means: You have a profound connection to goddess energy, particularly to Isis.

Expect an awakening and heightening of your intuitive abilities that will serve you well when it comes to making decisions.

You are faced with an important choice right now, so be sure to strike when the time is right, and don't hesitate when your gut tells you it's time.

Take some classes in kundalini yoga, and after a few classes, notice the difference in how this makes you feel."

"Keep your eyes and your senses open and alert, and don't be blinded by illusions perpetrated by others.

In the same book author Steven Farmer Ph.D. tells about what it means if cobra is our power animal: "You carry yourself with an air of nobility and dignity.

You have a gift of being able to look beyond the appearances of another person and into their soul, which can sometimes be intimidating to others.

You trust your instincts to dictate what you should do in any situation that's questionable or where there's any doubt.

You know when to withdraw and when to strike out."

Spirit Visitation

It wasn't until my grownup years that I developed a close relationship with Spirit Realm and was consciously aware of it. When it comes to angels I somehow had a belief that they are related to church and religion. Therefore there was not even a question about me believing in them as I didn't go to church. Even though Latvian folklore talks a lot about God mentioning many Gods, to me God was an old man with a long beard sitting on a cloud and watching down to Earth and I didn't really feel any connection with God in this sense. However I always knew there was more than there seemed to be because I knew there was a spirit realm.

The most significant spiritual moment happened one summer day when I was about 4 years old. I was running down the hill by our house and all there was to see was grass, flowers and trees in a background. Birds were singing and I could hear crickets. I was so taken by the beauty of it all and as I looked at butterflies playing in front of my eyes, I suddenly felt the absolute connectedness with all that there is, all was well and everything was just so perfect. It might seem small and simple experience yet it was so powerful and memorable.

Since I grew up as an only child in my family and neighborhood for the first 10 years of my life, I had quite a few imaginary friends. I never saw them with my physical eyes, but I always felt them, even when we didn't play. I had a feeling that someone was with me all the time and I feared it might be something evil. Have you ever had a feeling of someone following you? I felt it all the time. If I thought "I want to see it" I would then feel it taking form which was even scarier to me and made me think, "Run!".

Even though evenings and nights were my favorite part of the day because candlelight looked so beautiful, I now couldn't stand night anymore as I felt that invisible presence which was pretty scary. I just didn't allow myself to believe it could be something good, I didn't dare mention it to anyone, so the best way I coped - was singing or repeating in my mind, "I am safe and all is good! All is good and I am safe!"

As far as I was concerned bedtime was the worst as I could hear whispering and steps as if someone was walking. I remember once as I was already in high school, I had a sleepover, and as we turned off the light and were still chatting, I suddenly said to my friend – "Do you know that we are not alone here?" As soon as I said that, I saw several white silhouettes resembling humans without a face – leaning over my bed and me. That was the wildest thing ever. I was so scared and I kept screaming loudly – "we are alone, we are alone!"

I was always told what I did wrong and could not do anything to make my mom happy. Since she already was concerned about my weirdness, I didn't talk about my experiences. Although some strange things happened in our house that all of us experienced, like lights turning on and off by themselves, we heard footsteps, doors opening and closing but nobody was there. It was strange but at the same time very "normal" for our house and we accepted it.

A few years after moving into this house we found out that our house was built on a graveyard, which explained all these spirit visitations. It is still happening, according to my mom who still lives in the same house.

Power of Mind

There was a teacher in our school unlike the others. We thought she was weird because most of the time during her class she would tell us about her life story instead of talking about the subject. In 5th grade during one of her lessons she taught us to make our body fall asleep by saying: "I am asleep, I am asleep, my body is relaxed". She shared that the best idea would be to start from the tip of the toes visualizing the feet being relaxed, legs, and thighs all the way up to the head and mind. I was impressed. As soon as I got home I wanted to try it out. I lied down in my bed and started to visualize my body becoming relaxed and sleepy. The last thing I remember was my belly. I woke up half an hour later and was even more excited, as I knew now that it really works.

Now I became excited to learn about the possibilities of the mind. I started to look for books in the library, learn about meditation, even made some guided meditations myself and recorded them on a tape as listening to the words instead of visualizing helped me to focus more.

Being Accepted

When I moved to Germany a few weeks after graduating from the University of Latvia, I met people who also talked about magical things! My dream of a "little witch" was considered completely normal. They were playing with tarot cards and Osho cards. For Christmas I received my very first card deck – no surprise that on the card box it said – "Young Witch's Tarot Cards". I was so excited! What I had felt and experienced was actually real – there were other people around who also believed in magical and mystical things, other people who had similar experiences with spirit, people who thought that there was nothing wrong with being a witch. I loved it. The greatest thing I experienced was being accepted for who I was and what I had to say was as valuable as anyone else. It was such a new experience. I began to have hope for dreams coming true and it helped me to believe in myself. During almost two years that I lived there, I gained a great amount of confidence, a great amount of insight and knowledge that helped me to understand my earlier spiritual experiences and encouraged me to move forward. What helped me the most was that I was surrounded by people who accepted me for who I was.

I had heard about the Germans being perfectionists in everything. My experience was far from that. The people I was surrounded with were

56

easy going, easy to get along with. The family I lived with was the greatest ever! At the beginning I wasn't aware of the connection we had. The mom of the kids I was watching said that from the first moment she saw me, she felt a connection. I am so grateful she didn't give up trusting I'll "wake up" and feel it one day too. I remember people who didn't know our relationship often thought we were sisters; this confirmed our connection and strengthened my belief in it. We are definitely Soul Sisters. It has been almost ten years since we first met and experiences we have had together would fill a book.

Dreams Do Come True

(in Disney World)

My most significant "dreams coming true experience" started when I was about 12-13 years old - I was reading about Disneyland. Somehow I just knew I was going to visit Disneyland. I didn't know how, I didn't know when, but I knew I would. I remember myself saying "Even if it happens when I am old, I am still going to Disneyland one day!" The political situation in the country was not the most positive for traveling abroad; I wasn't good at speaking English, didn't have any plan how to afford it financially, but still deep down in my heart I knew that I would go to Disneyland.

When I first came to the United States, I lived in Michigan. Then later moved to Chicago and when things didn't work out there as well, I somehow knew the next place I would move to would be Florida.

I belonged to an Au-Pair program which had rules that didn't seem fair to me (of course people with elemental energy don't do rules well). I decided to take charge of my situation (break the rules) and found a way to move to Florida. Not in the Disney World area, but being in the same state was good enough. Moving to Florida came about within a month and from here going to Disney World was easier.

It was the most magical day of my life as I walked down the street in Disney World standing in front of Disney World's castle. My dream had come true more than ten years later but it sure was worth it to believe in my dream. I was in tears as I remembered the first picture of Disneyland I saw, the first feelings I had seeing and thinking about being there, and there I was. It didn't matter if I went on rides or not, what mattered to me was – I was here and so was my strong belief in miracles. I had evidence that dreams come true, which was like a miracle. I believe now more than ever that I can dream of anything I want and it will come true!

Dragons

Even when there was no other spiritual kind of information openly available, horoscopes were talked a lot about and of course, I was curious. I really liked dragons and when I found out that according to Chinese astrology I was born in the year of the dragon, it made sense. I felt like dragons have been misunderstood as many fairy tales and stories described dragons as "bad guys" and the ones that needed to be killed. I believed dragons were good and people just didn't want to see how good they were. I become quite obsessed with dragons and collected all the information and pictures I could find.

Years later while living in United States, I came across come dragon tarot cards. Those were the most beautiful and magical dragon pictures I had ever seen and I just had to get these cards. I loved them. I loved the energy of dragons; I loved the messages they brought, loved working with them. Coincidentally my boyfriend at the time was also into dragons. He even had a huge dragon tattoo on his back and also worked/ played with the same dragon cards (no such thing as coincidence, is there?!). I found that there were people who believe dragons were good, dragons doing positive for the world and helping everyone.

A couple years later when I moved to Scotland I came across the "Colourworks" color therapy system. I felt like I had to take the class to become a "Colourworks" practitioner and teacher myself. Only after I had taken the class, I found out about the existence of Dragon Essences/ Spritzers that were part of this "Colourworks" Therapy system. I was amazed!

("Colourworks")

This system described dragons as having powerful and beneficial messages for us. In the past people weren't ready to hear them, but now when we are shifting our consciousness, dragons are back to remind us of a higher dimensional truth of ourselves and Earth. At this time people are ready to listen and hear what dragons have to say and I am glad that they are acknowledged and accepted.

The day was filled with fun and dragon energy – black, golden, blue, green, white, cooper, red and pink. Each one of them had a different message as we channeled dragons and played with Dragon Essences. Their royal presence was felt in many different ways, we even experienced them playing with doors on the physical plane. My connection with dragons was deepened and our friendship was growing.

While visiting Laguna Beach, California, I spent a lot of time

("Dragon Rock" in Laguna Beach)

59

walking on the beach. As I came closer to what is known as "Manifestation Rock", I didn't see rock anymore. Instead I saw a dragon laying down on the beach. I was so fascinated to see the rock transform that hearing dragons talk to me at this point was less surprising.

I also saw a black dragon in the water that seemed to be just waiting to get my attention. I wasn't quite sure what it was and how it happened, but I felt other dragons approaching and looking at me. They said they wanted to be introduced to humanity through meditations and wanted me to write them down. I didn't know how to do this but they said that all I need to do is to sit down and be ready to write and they would do everything else.

For the next few weeks I would sit and be ready to write meditations from the dragons. They showed me images and guided me where to go during meditations.

At that time I also visited Sequoia National Park in central California. As I was driving in the park, I stopped to visit a waterfall in the mountains.

(Waterfall in Sequoia Park where I met dragons)

It was early morning and the sun was just coming out. I was drifting away with sounds of water and suddenly saw several dragons appear. They all were excited to talk and I could barely keep up with them. I learned that dragons represent the raw power; they want us to embrace our true power, believe in it, trust ourselves and don't give it to other

60

people and situations. I learned that they had to go into hiding, as humanity wasn't ready to take the responsibility in their hands and follow the ideas that dragons represented. People rely more on external sources than on the source within. They said those who knew about the inner power didn't want anyone else to know about it because they knew that people would remember that there is nothing to fear. So dragons were forced to hide as those in "power" tried to kill them. Every time people connected with dragons, they felt the power within them awakening and rising. It wasn't anything that the people with external power coming from ego wanted so dragons decided to wait for a shift of consciousness and come out then.

What amazing times we are living in now as this shift of consciousness is happening and we have the privilege of experiencing this new awakening.

Golden Dragon Meditation

(first meditation dragons shared with me)

Find a comfortable position and close your eyes. Inhale deeply and with every breath you take, feel your body filling with light, bringing peace. If you feel tension anywhere in your body, imagine (breathe in) light there and breathe out anything that you don't need anymore. Take your time.

See yourself in a beautiful place in the mountains. Feel the fresh air and fresh breeze, smell the flowers, listen to the sounds around you.

It's a sunny and bright day, butterflies are playing in the meadow, birds are singing ... look around and notice, what you see... know that with every breath you take, you become more and more relaxed, more and more in peace.

There is a fairy looking at you and she is asking you to follow her... and you get up and go with her. The fairy is leading you to a distant mountain, which looks majestic and mystical. The mountain is inside the mist and it doesn't seem easy to see, to understand, how big the mountain is, is there only one or more than one... seems like the mist is becoming stronger and stronger... you can't see the fairy anymore, but you feel her presence and you seem to know, where to go.

Suddenly bright golden light shoots out like a volcano from the top of the mountain, and you feel the excitement building, as you know you are

61

going right there. Even though you don't know what is happening what is awaiting you there, you feel safe. You are walking and walking and the mist is slowly disappearing... you find yourself standing on top of the mountain... there is a cave in front of you, which seems to lead you into another mountain, the same mountain, which just a little while ago was shooting golden light... and the fairy is asking you to follow her. You feel the excitement building and building... and you follow the fairy into the cave. The fairy's light is showing you the way... you feel the freshness coming from the cave, strong breeze coming from inside the mountain... feel your belly, feel the energy building up in your solar plexus area... you can see the light at the end of the cave... you are almost there...

The closer you get to the light, the more you feel very strong energy coming from it. The most magnificent view opens up, when you get at the end of the cave ... you see where the light is coming from and where the shooting light is coming from. There is a dragon... a golden dragon inside a mountain... his body is shining so bright; his energy is so vibrant and strong that you are amazed. Your eyes meet and you greet each other... The dragon has a deep and magical look in his eyes and his presence makes you feel safe and well protected.

Dragons wish for mankind to extend their spiritual knowledge to include and accept the dragon's existence and purpose as they have much wisdom to offer. The time has come for you to connect with these majestic beings, the dragons.

Just stay in his presence, take in this energy... make a connection with this dragon and listen for any message or messages for you... feel that intense power offered by this dragon and notice this power being activated within you... ask the dragon (in your mind) if there is anything you need to know at this moment, this time... or ask him any question that comes to your mind...

Then golden dragon is holding you safe and taking you for a ride... you are flying out through the top of the mountain and it is truly an amazing ride. He is showing you your past life times when you had fully claimed your own personal, true power. He is helping you recall moments from those life times so you can believe how powerful and amazingly wonderful you are!!!

Take in the experience.

Finally dragon is bringing you back home, back to the place where you started the journey... back to the present moment. You thank Golden Dragon for the experience and you both know you are going to think of each other and recall the sacred time together.

You return back into the room a more powerful and confident person than you have ever been!

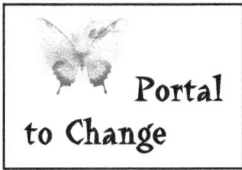

Portal to Change	*Every spiritual experience, big or small, is valuable and takes a significant part in everyone's life journey!*
	What are your most significant spiritual experiences?

CHAPTER III

Out of our Greatest Challenges come the Greatest Gifts

Being Made Fun of – an Everyday Experience

Even though I knew everyone was different, I felt like I was more unique. I wanted to fit in so badly. I wanted to belong somewhere, I wanted to be part of something however each time I tried I was even more misunderstood and left out.

It began in my family where I felt my mom was doing the best she could to love me, but still she wanted me to be someone else. I often felt like I was dropped off from another planet, totally foreign to my environment and unable to fit in or belong.

I saw other children at school who seemed to be "normal" and I so wanted to be like them, I wanted to have friends. I felt if I would be like others, all would be well. I also had this feeling that people around me expected me to be someone else but since nobody said how they wanted me to be, I just did my best to please everyone the best way I could. I agreed with everything said, I thought that something was wrong with me if I didn't think or did as others; I adopted other people's beliefs and manners and made them mine. I wanted to wear (never really did) similar clothes as others as I felt like I would gain acceptance. I even made fun of myself just to be part of the group and feel like I belonged.

No matter how I was and what I did, deep inside I hated my life. I felt trapped and desperate to be accepted. There was no way to avoid being laughed at and teased every day to my extreme despair.

I have somehow managed to delete details from my memory about the very painful moments in my life as that has seemed to be the best way to cope. It's completely surprising to me but when I think of my life in school up till college, I have mostly negative memories and a few significant events to support my painful feelings. In my desperation I was trying to be someone else at the same time pretending to be different as long as it was positive thing (I'll talk about it later in this chapter), feeling embarrassed, helpless and wanting to die.

I know my mom did the best she could when she went to see my teacher about challenges she had with me at home, but the result was that my teacher made sure the whole class found out what was talked about and if I had any feeling of being safe there it was gone at that point. I was laughed at for who and how I was, I was laughed at because my mom talked to the teacher and no other parent had done that, I was laughed at for not having a dad - I was humiliated because of my family and where I came from.

Major teasing started after my teacher had seen me playing with two boys during the weekend. She mentioned it during the class on the next day of school and called me a name that means something similar to "she who sleeps around with different men". I was ten years old at the time and the boys were my cousins who had come to visit but that didn't matter to anyone. For a few years this lovely name was adopted by other classmates, which made me cry almost every day at school. I couldn't go to the teacher for support as she was the one who called me this in the first place and all I could think of doing was crying and feeling worse and worse about life. I felt my life was so unfair. Other kids found more reasons to make fun of me for almost anything such as my eyes or the way I looked.

I felt like I knew what the real truth was but I believed my life to be the worst thing ever as I seemed to attract people who "attacked" me everywhere I went.

After we moved to live in a city when I was ten years old, the girl from a nearby house I didn't know, made fun of me or bullied me every time I saw her (on the street when she was with her friends). Another girl whose name I didn't know either told me if I looked at her one more time, she would hit me in the face. A woman who was at least 3 or 4 times my age, who sat on the same bus I took to go to school, threatened me the same way. (I found out later that she was once in love with my dad when my mom went out with him). Getting on the bus was a terrifying thing for me. A man on the bus kept staring at me and few times asked me to go out with him. He was a great looking man and since I didn't know what happened to my dad, who he was and where he was, I imagined this man was my dad who found me at last. However, his look was too creepy and I was scared of him.

With the understanding I have now these situations are examples of how we attract similar situations no matter where we go if we allow them to take over our whole being.

The way it was, I didn't see any reason to live and often drifted into a dream world of how great it would be if I were dead. I gave a lot of thought to the best way to end my life, what would be easiest and least painful. Luckily, I never had the courage to actually do it.

Focusing on Passion

* In Latvia the only way to take music lessons was to go to a music school: pass exams to be accepted at first, besides the main instrument anyone wanted to learn to play (lessons were twice a week) all students had to take piano lessons (once a week), history of music, class that taught to read, write and recognize notes, sing in a choir (twice a week)... every semester – 4 times a year every student had to take and pass an exam in a main instrument to be able to continue studies. Depending on the instrument the student was learning to play, the studies continued 5 to 8 years the main instrument I chose to learn was piano (8 years program)

When I was about 12 years old things started to change. I was fascinated by the guitar when I first saw a teachers play it. I knew it was something I wanted to do. Even though I went to a music school since age 6 (see*) and learned to play the piano, I found much more joy at the thought of playing guitar and singing. Even though I was extremely shy, my fascination with the guitar was stronger so I walked up to the teacher to ask if she would teach me to play. I was over the clouds when she agreed. Pretty soon I was playing the guitar and performing in all school events which expanded into performing in other schools and events in the area. My guitar teacher put together a group of 6 students, with two of us playing guitar and all of us singing. I convinced my only friend in school into singing duet with me. Soon we performed everywhere singing popular songs as well as original songs that I wrote myself. Now I had something fun to focus on; I became devoted to my music and passion of performing. **Out of my greatest misery came the greatest gift.**

More or less I had given up the idea to be like everyone else and loved the fact that I was the only student in school who played the guitar. I also seemed to have gained some respect from others and was left alone. I didn't gain more friends nor was I invited to be part of some group but the teasing had finally ended which was a great relief.

I went to 3 different schools up until I started college and in all of them I was the only one who played the guitar, sang and performed my music. I loved this kind of "different" as it helped me to build my confidence. I was still considered a weirdo and throughout all my school years had only few good friends, but I had found a way to break through the old pattern, I had found a positive way to be different.

(one of our regular "Stair concerts" in Latvia)

The memories of being laughed at were still strong and talking in front of a group of people was terrifying. I was afraid I would say something that would cause people to laugh at me so I preferred to express myself with my music.

For 5 years I went to college and during that time I studied music as much as possible. I was studying in the city that was considered to be most musical city in the country and I chose a college based on musical reasons. Once there I found a way to contact the woman who was the "mother" of singers/songwriters and folk music in Latvia. For several years I studied with her. We were invited to perform throughout the country as a group as well as I was getting solo gigs. I had found acceptance through expressing myself in a positive way; I had found something positive to focus on and do in my life.

Even though I felt like I had found the way to deal with life, deep inside I knew that there was more to it: more to let go, more to embrace but for the time being I was pretty happy with the way things were.

"This Girl will Need to Work Hard"

One of the greatest challenges in my life has been to live in prosperity: to allow it in my life, to accept it, to claim it.

My mom said, "This girl knows that she will need to work hard and make her way in life on her own," as I surprised her by walking at the age of 9 months. I don't know if mom was serious when she said it but she was absolutely correct.

How important is work in my life's journey? No matter from which side you look – I grew up knowing what having a job and working hard was about, all aspects of it.

Taken from Latvian Folklore: "The value of work, or the work ethic, has been held in particularly high esteem by Latvians. It most likely grew out of the northern environment, where nature offers little without hard work, and therefore "work is life.""

All my life I heard how hard it was to earn money, and the more we work the more money we get for our work. I had many years of experience and proof for this to be true as well. Firstly – there was always a lot to do on our farm as we had quite a few animals. We also had a huge vegetable garden that yielded a great amount of vegetables that we stored in the cellar so we could have plenty to eat throughout the whole winter, about 20 apple trees and my favorite – strawberries (in summer time I picked a bucket full of strawberries every other day), black and red currants. Also to mention – as we lived in the middle of the woods, summertime was when we went to the woods to pick up blueberries, raspberries, cranberries and mushrooms.

(mushrooms)

Different herbs were also something we picked up from early spring till late summer as each one of them was ready to be picked in different times.

We made our own jam and marmalade, pickles, sauerkraut, apple juice... We also had a beautiful flower garden around the house with flowers blooming from early spring till late fall. Grass needed to be cut all year long except winter and there was no such thing as a lawn mower – we did it the old fashioned way with a scythe. Now, those were all things that were necessary to do, they were part of our every day life and we didn't know any different and it involved quite a lot of work. I have to admit, some of this work was fun, like going to the woods, picking blueberries and eating them freshly picked our hands and teeth would turn blue and it took few days to be able to wash it all off, so we would walk around "blueberry blue". I loved to overcome challenges and one them was to find the best mushroom hiding places. I mastered that pretty quickly and it was (still is, when I go to visit as my family still owns the same house) so much fun to find mushrooms as they are never in the same place as before. I always loved to walk in the woods and listen to the birds singing, see the wind blowing in the trees and breathe the fresh air that is super clean there. Often I would just sit down and drift into my dream world while out in the woods and let it soothe my soul and regenerate my spirit.

(there was always work to do...)

I always had my "imaginary" friends with me when I was out in woods – they were the best company that I could wish for and helped me to feel safe. I didn't think this was something special at the time. Now I realize what a gift these days spent in nature were to my survival.

I began my first job for money when I was only 8 years old. There were many jobs to do during summer. In the Soviet Union, everything belonged to the community. In my village there was more work to do in the summer than during the winter and children were asked and allowed to work. We picked weeds, cut weeds, stocked bricks, helped collect hay for community farms, shepherded cows and worked in community farms. Throughout the years, I did all of it. I started out picking weeds, then moved to shepherding cows which was the greatest challenge for me because it required waking up early. I am a born "night owl" but this job required me to wake up at 4AM. I was 10 years old at the time and even waking up at 7AM for school seemed too early for me. From all the work I did throughout the years, stocking hay was the easiest thing as we could rest after one truck was emptied until the next one came. Also it was very rewarding to harvest sugar beets as we got paid for it and got extra sugar. It was great to have this extra sugar in order to make tasty sweet jellies.

At the age of 16 my summer work was picking blueberries and selling them. Every other day I would get up with the sun to go to the woods for berries, then spent the afternoons cleaning the leaves off. The next morning I walked with a bucket in each hand filled with blueberries 6 miles to the closest bus station that took me to the city where berries could be sold.

I wasn't the only child who worked. We didn't know any different, kids worked all summer and I liked to earn my own money. Since I went to

71

music school, I paid for it myself with money I earned during summer and was very proud to be able to do it.

Usually I invested the rest of my money in some sweets throughout the rest of year - it was my pocket money. There wasn't much else to buy anyway. I really wanted to have a tape player (we didn't know such things as CDs and CD players existed), but we had a wait list for tape recorders. According to where we were on this list as well as how often the store got recorders in stock, we could buy them. I guess I was in a line at the very bottom as my turn never came.

Life was pretty simple – but since we didn't know any different, it wasn't a big deal. However once the country got independent things changed and we were introduced to more and more new and exciting things and foods. All kinds of things were suddenly available for everyone. We went through several monetary changes and even though my family had always had enough money for all we needed, as a result of the changes, our family was in a lower economic class. We started to have major struggles with money and whereas it didn't make any logical sense, we seemed to get poorer with every year. The economy was in a transformation, which made things worse for us.

My most challenging financial struggle was during college. Luckily, I passed the exams well and got accepted in a budget group which meant I didn't have to pay for my studies, however everything else required payment.

This was the time I started to hitchhike as a way to get from home to school and back. I discovered that even though that was the only way for me to be able to afford to stay in school and save on bus fare, hitchhiking was fun. I would meet all kinds of people and many of them would also buy me a meal if they decided to stop and have some lunch on the way (it was about 6 hour drive from my home to University). It sure helped me with my situation. As I was into music a lot, I promised all the people who took me in their car when I was hitchhiking, that I would acknowledge them on my first album.

Working was not an option as at that point with all the changes happening in Latvia, people my age got jobs if they knew someone on a personal level who could hire. I didn't know anyone and I actually didn't know how I could work as school was 5 days a week starting at 8AM and often ending at 5PM or even later with lots of homework at night if we wanted to pass and move forward with studies.

Students got a minimal monthly allowance of - $20. $10 of that went to rent for the shared room which left only $10 for food and other needs. The last two years in college were extremely challenging as prices went up for everything but the allowance stayed the same. I remember often spending 2-3 days without food as I didn't have any money to buy some. I learned that drinking hot water tricked my body to feel like I had something to eat. I would go window shopping for food, imagining I was eating what I saw and this visualization helped. There were a lot of tricks I learned from this experience – spiritual and practical.

Even though I got into a very pessimistic state, using visualization where I saw myself having food to eat, having boots that didn't have holes (I used to put my feet in plastic bags and then in boots so my feet would stay dry on rainy days and I wouldn't get cold), dreaming of the happy place and space I wanted to be helped me to live.

Even though thoughts of killing myself came back it was like someone was stopping me from doing it. I did have major sleeping problems and regularly got ill with something – luckily it was nothing major, just a cold, sore throat, runny nose which eventually turned into pneumonia, and an unexplainable fever of 105 for several months. I knew I needed some help for my mind to get clear, as I believed all these physical problems were coming from financial challenges I had and thoughts that were related to them. I ended up with needing to take 5-6 sleeping pills and having regular psychotherapist visits. Pills helped me for a while but I learned that talking was what helped me the most. I was looking forward to have these visits as they helped me to feel that things could change, I knew it was a therapists job to listen – but it really helped me to feel like what I felt and experienced mattered. I did feel like I was existing, not living, but even though I didn't have the conscious belief in God or Angels, or anything spiritual at this point in my life, I did have the feeling of someone looking out for me no matter what happened. I had a feeling that all would be ok, that something better is coming. I became more and more aware of the loving presence of someone looking after me.

We Are All Equal

One day my friend excitingly was telling about a program she had found – Au-Pair, a program that allowed girls of certain age to be like a big sister to a family in a foreign country, providing living space, food, language classes and some extra cash. I was excited by this idea and the possibility of leaving my country was making my heart sing. I didn't know how it would actually happen but I was extremely disappointed in my home country and my life and I wanted to get far, far away from it all.

My travels started during the last year of college. I headed to Sweden for my first experience living abroad. It was the beginning of my next journey. Even though my first experience wasn't so great, seeing that life could be different from what I had experienced was something I was very grateful for. It was much easier to learn English which had always been a great challenge for me in school. I saw what a completely different environment could do. I also saw how much more there was to life than I ever knew. I was in love with traveling and with living abroad because I could experience life from an everyday point of view instead of as a tourist. I got to see the foreign country for what it was, I got to see it from a local person's point of view: all the ups and downs, family life, work and fun, and prosperity which even though wasn't mine helped me to feel prosperous myself.

I returned to Latvia to finish my studies and a couple weeks after graduation, moved to Germany. I didn't speak German at all but my willingness to experience life in this country was greater than worries about the language. Living abroad enabled me to discover who I was and realize how much power I had within. I did things I never really dreamt of doing: I learned to speak English fluently and learned a few other languages besides – Swedish and German. I learned that I could make friends, I learned that I could find my way around wherever I went. I had a chance to learn from an abusive situation *(see the next chapter)* during an experience abroad as a way to let go of my old behaviors that were not working anymore.

Releasing the Old

"Au pairs are caring, live-in childcare providers who live as an extended member of their host family and provide childcare for up to 10 hours per day and 45 hours per week in USA (different in each country). Au pairs are between the ages of 18 and 26. In exchange for providing childcare, au pairs receive room, board, and a small stipend."

When I went to live in Sweden I was invited to be with a family with 5 children. They had one nanny already and their application/letter said that they were looking for a weekend nanny (in Sweden Au-pair was meant to provide childcare up to 25 hours a week), which meant working two days and having 5 days to do other things. The family offered their nanny her own apartment and Swedish language classes. It sounded good to me and I agreed to go. I was so excited and open to new experiences!

Soon after arriving I learned the real truth about this offer and my responsibilities. The "promised" apartment was a room in the family's business office that I had to share with another nanny. There was a man who was renting another room in this "apartment" who didn't know about our existence, but we had to share the same bathroom – which meant us sneaking in without him noticing us. It wasn't that hard as he was mostly working during night and home during the day.

I was asked to take care of the children in the family's house every weekday from 3pm-9pm. Even though I had the morning off, I had to be out of the "apartment" before 8am as that's when people came to work and the family didn't want anyone in the office to know anyone lived there. So from 8am – 3pm I had to find something to do somewhere else.

When it came to weekends the family went to their summer house on an island. By 8am Saturday morning I had to be in the family house and we all got in the car to drive there which took about 2 hours. My room was in separate building with one bed, lamp and a chair. Bathroom use for an Au-pair was outside and the shower – on the boat. My responsibilities were to take care of the 3 youngest children from the moment the youngest one got up (around 6am Sunday) till they all went to bed around 9pm. Then the most shocking part to me was following: The parents had a party every Saturday night and my responsibility was to prepare everything for the party, during the party be like a bartender – bring drinks, snacks, take away dirty dishes, etc. The first Saturday I was there I went to bed around midnight (which was actually Sunday morning already) knowing that the little one woke up around 6AM.

I was awakened by the furious mom in the middle of the night and had no idea what happened. It was 3 o'clock in the morning and turned out that the party guests had just left. I was expected to clean up right at that very moment.

The biggest shock for me was yet to come. I was not physically able to work 18 hours one day, have about 3 hours of sleep and then work another 15 hours. Each week on workdays I worked 6 hours a day and had to wander around elsewhere because I was not allowed to stay "home". It was so unfair and I was angry and sad at the same time. I had just arrived in the country and I liked it there, but living and working conditions were worse than I could have ever pictured them.

I asked if I would get paid more since I was working almost 3 times more than the Au-pair program allows. My greatest shock was the dad's response: "You come from a former Soviet Union country, you don't have any right to ask for something. You must do what you are told and obey, those are the rules. Did you really think that you would be treated as any of us?"

Yes, I really did. I did believe as this program was supposed to be culture exchange program where all sides involved learn & teach. My intuitive (indigo) self knew and felt this to be unfair. This wasn't some kids from neighborhood or school teasing me, this was worse than that. At this point I wasn't consciously aware that any situation in our life is because we have created it ourselves. From my new perspective as a world traveler I believed that we are all equal and I wanted to feel that in my life everywhere I went. I decided that no matter where I went, no matter what I did, where I worked, what position I was in, I would be treated equally. I had this feeling that part of my mission was to show by example that it didn't matter where we came from, what color our skin was, no matter what language we spoke, what our financial situation was, what our religion was, we were all equal as humans, we all have unique mission in life and none of them is less important or less valuable than another.

Spiritual Awakening

As soon as I came to the USA a couple years later, I felt like I was meant to be there. Everything in the USA fascinated me.

After several unsuccessful placements in families as an au-pair, I broke some rules (this is where my indigo-fairy-wise one (more about it in chapter V) personality showed up to help me) and I found a great family to live with in Florida.

(Our TROUBLE team - it says on my shirt "watch out, here comes trouble and on girls shorts - "trouble")

76

Soon I started to become more aware of spirituality as so many possibilities and opportunities were around. I found all kinds of things related to what was called "New Age". Most interesting for me was witches and witchcraft as I always wanted to be a little witch after all. I signed up for a class called "Craft 101" and only then found out that it was actually "Witchcraft 101". I was so excited to learn about such things and I truly felt like I belonged. Of course I had to try out different spells and take part in some rituals that I found to be very interesting even though I could never remember what came after what during the ritual, I was fascinated to live my childhood's dream and learn that there were many like minded people. How could I not love it? I felt like I had found a great part of me that was missing.

For the whole time living there I was very much involved in what I call the "witchy" life: I attended different rituals, celebrations, played with my dragon and angel cards, practiced magic on my own and in the group. I also attended Body, Mind, Spirit Expo every time it took a place in the area and was quickly absorbing all I felt drawn to from these events. It made my heart sing and that's all that mattered – I loved to feel my heart singing!

In one of the local spiritual stores, I saw a picture of a Stone Circle which wakened an "old memory"! I felt called to go to this place with the stone circles. I knew I had to go and that was the reason I started to look for an opportunity to move to Ireland as I thought Ireland was the place where Stone Circles were.

I moved back to Latvia and began to look for work in Ireland. Instead I was offered a job in Scotland. I had never actually heard about Scotland nor had I any intention to visit, but I figured Scotland is close to Ireland, I'll take this opportunity.

Can you imagine my surprise when I walked into a tourist information center in Scotland to find a leaflet of places of interest and an exact picture of the Stone Circle I saw in Florida? Suddenly I got "angel" bumps throughout my body and at that point I knew that I was in the right place. *(My spiritual experiences while here are in Chapter V).*

Compared to my lonely childhood, traveling provided me some great friendships and connections with people from almost 20 different countries, so far. I love having friends just as much as I enjoy being one.

I see myself "being different" no matter where I am. I am different when I live abroad because of where I come from and experiences I have had in different countries. When I go back to Latvia, I am different there too for the very same reason. Yet, I am grateful to be so unique and actually enjoy it!

The greatest lesson my travels have brought me is the lesson of self-acceptance and the acceptance of others. I saw how different the places we come from are, how different the culture, how different are people's beliefs and actions, yet it all fits together perfectly. There is no good or bad, there is just different.

Portal to Change

As I mentioned above, everyone is different and each one of us has our own path to take and live. Challenges help us grow and learn and we all experience them. Some of them are bigger some smaller. When we see challenges as an opportunity to grow, it's easier to overcome them.

What are the most challenging situations you have experienced in your life? What lessons have you learned through these experiences?

How have they (the lessons) helped you to be the person you are now?

CHAPTER IV

My Yoga Journey

When we change inside – the world around us changes.

"I have to go to the library to return some books, will you come with me?" asked my only and best friend. "Sure, what books were you reading?" I was curious. My friend handed me the books she was holding. "Yoga for life." "What is that about?" I asked. "Oh, there are only exercises, no stories and not so interesting," my friend replied.

I didn't know why I had the feeling of recognition as I was looking at the cover of this book. I knew that I had to read it! If only I would have brought back my books as we could only have 2 books at a time from the school library and I had my two at home. The librarian was really nice and since I had always brought books back in time, she made an exception and let me take the "yoga" book home. That's when my yoga journey started. I was 10 years old and even my most favorite story books didn't give me such an exciting feeling as this one. I was "eating" the book – I felt so "hungry" for all the content of "yoga for life". There were different sets of poses for improving different areas of life, each pose had a description - how to do it and the benefits of each. I was so fascinated by it I started to practice right away. I closed the door to my room, so nobody could see me (shyness + fear of being disapproved). The lion pose was the first one I did as it was said that it improves the voice and singing was one of my main passions. I had my tongue out as far as it went and then made a roaring sound. Moment by moment my "roaring" voice become stronger and I became more comfortable with my practice. Several hours later I went through almost all poses until I finally had enough for the first day.

I still didn't know how to put it in words, but yoga felt so familiar to me. From that day on every day I spent hours practicing poses. I even put together my own set of poses for things I wanted to improve in my life. I was also very busy copying the book. There was no such thing as a copy machine in our country at that time so I had to handwrite and draw pictures of the poses. I had only one week to finish until the book had to be returned. I had never been so determined in my whole life to finish something as I was with this project.

When the weather was nice I would go outside and live my "yogi" life there. My mom and grandma had seen me practice yoga already inside and they were concerned that I would break some bones holding these "weird" poses. Since our house was surrounded by trees and bushes I was unseen by the outside world and I found the practice outdoors to be more profound than doing it in my room. I was holding many poses for 10-15 minutes as I noticed the longer I held the slower my breathing got and the more flexible I became. I just loved the feeling that holding poses gave me and how the practice made me feel afterwards. It was like I had "gained" lightness every time I "played" with yoga. I also liked being able to go deeper in pose than before. "I can, I can, I can" – I heard as my whole being celebrated excitingly.

(me in backbend)

I was already considered to be weird and laughed at school so I didn't share my new interest with anyone. But I did feel proud of myself for finding something that gave me excitement and made me feel good, I was also proud of myself for being flexible. In "sport" class we had to practice splits and back bends and it was part of our exam. I was top of the class in flexibility tests. I had found something to look forward to and felt more relaxed in all I did, everywhere I went. Those who were the biggest teasers must have noticed as teasing me got less interesting for them and eventually turned into a neutral relationship (credit for that to my other passion – music - as well, see Chapter V). At that time I didn't understand why that had happened, but looking back I can see that this was my first experience and proof that **when we feel good about what we do, even if there is only one part of our life that we feel good about, the world around us changes.**

I kept practicing yoga daily for about 5 years until singing gigs changed my focus, but that is another story to come.

15 Years Later...

I decided to practice yoga again as I could hear Spirit's loud messages urging me. I would pull a "yoga" card as guidance for just about any question I asked Spirit. I would hear it in my head and yoga ads would "jump" out when I looked at magazines. After resisting for a while I gave in and promised myself to go back to yoga. I began to consider all the different yoga studios around. Then it came to mind that it would be Laguna Beach, as it was the closest city to where I lived at the time. From the moment I found the studio things went wild. I believe my angels were making sure I went where I was meant to.

I signed up for a two week trial, which allowed me to access all the yoga studio branches in the local area with hundreds of different classes available for exploration. I wanted to find the right class, one I could really enjoy and look forward to. I checked out the class schedule for different classes to see if any caught my attention. The class that was said to have live music "jumped" out most of all. It was in a city that I had never heard of, but since it was within the same county, it couldn't be so far, could it?

So here I was, driving to my first yoga class. Incredibly, almost all the traffic lights were green and I got to the studio in less time than my printed directions indicated.

Right away I felt something special about this studio. The class was amazing and very similar to what I practiced as a child: holding poses for several minutes, deep stretching together with wisdom quotes for the soul plus guitar music, cello and crystal bowl sounds.

Here is a little story with some photos that is a diversion from the yoga subject, but is very significant looking at the bigger picture in my further journey.

I have been very blessed to have spirit and orbs show themselves on my pictures quite a few times. The most recent one was in the picture that was taken at the "Cairo Belly Dance Festival". As I was showing it to my friends, most of them were saying that this spirit looks a lot like the sitting Buddha.

See for yourself:

(me & orb in a shape of sitting Buddha)

This idea resonated with me and I was very excited and grateful to be supported and visited by Spirit. Little did I know at the time that Buddha's image on the photo was more significant than I thought.

At the end of this wonderful yoga class, I walked up to the teacher to thank her for the great class and almost froze for a moment. There was a sitting Buddha statue in front of the class that I hadn't noticed before. I suddenly got lovely angel "bumps" - as I describe the chills - all over my body and it all clicked together. In a flash, I saw the picture with a spirit and sitting Buddha emerge together, all the yoga cards and messages come together and I knew for sure that this was the right studio and the right class for me. Besides, I had learned in the past that it's important for me to feel the connection with a teacher, no matter what kind of class it would be, the connection I felt with the teacher of this class was unique, even though I couldn't pinpoint what exactly the significance was.

I noticed after about the 4th or 5th time I drove to this yoga studio that every time I would get the green traffic lights. I counted 29 traffic lights between my house and the yoga studio. I was amazed to get only 3 red lights at the most when I went to yoga class. I even did a little experiment – I drove to the same city for other reason than yoga and got "stuck" at the red lights more often. However when I went to yoga I hit almost all green lights. It was like the angels were making sure that my way to yoga was as easy as possible since they knew the benefits I would get from it.

The next class I took in this studio was Kundalini yoga. Being aware of the spiritual side of life, I knew about Kundalini energy and I had no doubt this class would be very beneficial for all aspects of my life.

Besides all the yoga benefits, I gained the greatest friends. Thanks to one of the teachers of this class, I started to play the guitar in one of the other classes in this studio through which I gained even more friends and opportunities.

(teacher Karta Singh & me... at yin yoga class)

One other interesting thing – as I was dreaming about my house, I always knew there wouldn't be chairs in my living room, only pillows. I didn't know why, but I wanted lots of pillows to sit on. I suddenly realized, during a Snatam Kaur concert, that we all sat on our yoga mats and yoga pillows. With this realization came greater understanding and clarity about my connection with Kundalini yoga.

I was most passionate about the first class I took in this studio, as the practice awoke some part of me on a deeper level than ever before. This practice also helped me to connect with my inner child, brought wonderful memories and being present gave me a positive boost for the future. Very often, I would think of something I would like to work on spiritually during the class, I would walk into the class and the teacher would bring our awareness and focus exactly on what I had wanted to work on. I felt the universe was giving me confirmation after confirmation of the importance of this practice in my life and it's benefits. It's how the universe confirms that we are in the right place meeting the right people and teachers.

I realized that **when we are more focused and working from the heart, our best is better when we are in the presence of certain situations and certain people. Our connecting energy (with certain people) helps to invoke something real and true within us, which helps us to be more who we are and to believe we can do anything.** Yoga practice in class mentioned above has had exactly this effect on my life's journey and spiritual growth.

Past Life Connection

The more time passed I experienced more connection with the teacher of this yoga class. If at the beginning I thought it was just a coincidence that she would pick the same intention for the class than I did (without me sharing it with her) then after 3rd or 4th time I was not so sure about it anymore. In fact, I was sure about opposite – I was sure we were spiritually connected in some way. It was confirmed to me when I was shown a vision during meditation in the very same class. I was shown (when I say "shown" - I receive messages from spirit by seeing them in my mind's eye like a movie) a temple, us inside the temple meditating. There was a group of people, about 7, and we were all practicing levitation, something I would love to do in this life. It was interesting but I still couldn't make a clear connection.

More time passed and some important event happened in this particular teacher's life. She left the yoga studio I went to and coincidentally, the opening of her new studio was exactly on my birthday. I was even more surprised when I found out that it was her birthday too.

Even though by that time I had experienced many interesting things happen, many synchronicities and many miraculous events – this connection was way beyond my "usual" experience. I turned to my spirit friends asking for some insights and guidance regarding this connection with my teacher. What I was shown seemed so simple that I disregarded it at first – I was shown us being twins in a past life. I was looking for confirmation about the vision and connected with a Past Life Regression Therapist. Without me sharing any information about the vision I saw, the therapist confirmed we had been twin sisters in a past life. On the soul level we remember our close connection which made it easy to communicate telepathically in this lifetime. Our mystical birthday "coincidence" was meant to help us to remember this connection and it sure did for me. After receiving the confirmation, I was shown the moment in my past life where we took the vow to meet in this lifetime. We were sitting opposite each other by the fire, holding hands while levitating just above the fire flame and made a promise to find each other in this life. Interesting was the fact that in all the visions about our past life together that I was shown, we communicated telepathically. I was also shown that my passion for twins in this lifetime comes as a result of remembering having a twin sister on a soul level. A few days after this "discovery" I was doing yoga poses outside in the back yard. As I got comfortable into pose I heard (in my mind) this teacher's voice telling me what to focus on in this particular pose, how to hold my hands, where to turn my head – it was like me having a private yoga lesson for the whole time of my practice. How amazingly cool is that? It didn't end there as I thought it would. I took the same type of class with a different teacher and the same thing happened again. Besides what the teacher in front of the class said, my "sister" guided me into poses throughout the class.

Following My Intuition

A couple weeks past since the opening of the new yoga studio. Even though I decided to wait a few weeks before I signed up for the classes there, one day I woke up with the strong feeling that the right time is "now". It was as if this feeling had taken over my whole being and I had no other choice than to sign up for the classes. Since I wasn't sure what it was about, I purchased the smallest package - 10 classes and was excitingly waiting for the class.

The next day after my first class in this studio, late at night I was working on my website when suddenly my ear got hot (every time somebody talks about me, my ear feels like burning and literally becomes red). I was "taken away" from my work and shown (the same way I receive intuitive messages) this teacher sending me a message. It was sent out in a thought form and arrived to me in an envelope. I opened the envelope, took out the letter... I only saw my name on it but couldn't see clearly what the rest of the letter said. However, I saw pink and golden colors with it. I felt guided to e-mail her about this experience, as my ear kept "burning" stronger. The feeling was the same that guided me to sign up for the classes in the new studio. I argued with my angels a little bit as I wasn't sure if it was such a good idea to tell her about this experience however, I had already learned that there was no point in arguing with angels for too long and I gave in. I sent the e-mail. Next morning there was another class by this teacher and again, I wasn't planning on taking it, but the angels urged me to go. I did and was happy I listened. I found out that the teacher really had sent me a message the day before. The following week she was going to move to a different state and was not going to teach in this particular studio anymore. The place she was going to move would allow her to see the golden sunsets and the work place had exact colors as the ones I received with the message in my vision as well. She was offered this new opportunity around the same time I felt guided to sign up for classes. I was amazed! Now it also made sense to me why I was guided to purchase only a smallest pack age as my 10 class "trial" would enable me to go to all the classes this teacher would teach in this particular studio before moving.

This was again a clear example of how **situations amazingly unfold when we follow step by step the guidance we are given.** I did feel that this validation and realization had lifted my spirit once again to a new and higher vibrating level. This is exactly what I had experienced already before and knew to be true: no matter what we believe in, Spirit world, the Universe, God – they all celebrate with us our trust in guidance we receive and action we take as a result, and gift us abundantly with a higher sense of clarity and allow us to see the magic that is around us.

I knew I was guided to go to yoga to start with, but my experiences have gone beyond my expectations!

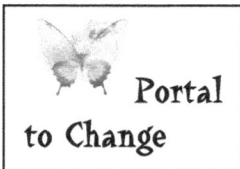

Portal to Change

Even though my experience with the yoga class was unique to me you also have had different experiences that are significant to you, which can be anything as "small" as a feeling, words said, action taken, a book read that held meaning or purpose later. Remember there is no such thing as a right or wrong way! All is right and in divine perfect order or "meant to be."

Think of one of your significant childhood experiences that made sense/ came together later as you grew up?

CHAPTER V

Angels Making Themselves Known

(my angel friend & me)

Growing up, I never thought about angels. I believed that angels were only in the church and since I grew up in a non-religious family there was no way of me getting in touch with angels.

My life changed once I moved to USA. For one thing I learned to love shopping. I had never seen so many great things in one place, so many different types of clothes and I had never seen such a huge variety in stores as I did there.

Here is where angels made their presence known for the first time. For some reason I felt extremely drawn to everything with angel wings, pictures of angels, the word "angel" and the halo. There was no logical reason why I would like angels – I just felt drawn to them and bought a lot of angelic things.

My next experience was at a Body, Mind and Spirit Fair that I went to when I lived in Florida. I came across a "Healing with Angels" card deck by Doreen Virtue Ph.D and I was given clear guidance to buy the deck. I wasn't sure about it but I chose to go with my intuition. I didn't know anything about the author and her work nor anything about angels, but since I had angel cards now, I was playing with them every day (when I say "play" I mean, I used them). They helped me set an intention for the day and I liked the energy of cards as well as the whole process of pulling cards.

At the same fair, I noticed a woman who I found out later was a spiritual counselor working with the angelic realm. I felt drawn to make an individual appointment with her. The truth is during the session I didn't believe that it was angels giving her messages even though she was right about everything. More than anything I believed that she was just intuitively reading me.

I did indeed feel presence of spiritual beings with me increasing but I didn't really know what it was.

It wasn't until I moved to Scotland a couple of years later that I came across angels once again.

Time Warping With Archangel Metatron

In the same "Colourworks" class that I made a connection with dragons, I also learned more about angels. This Color Therapy system had "Angel essences" as part of it. As we talked about each essence and the angel representing it I started to understand more about angels than I had known before. Some of the other students shared stories of angels and even though it didn't seem quite real to me, I was open to learn more. In discussion the teacher explained that Metatron (his essence is the color magenta) helps to stop the time. She shared a story of how Metatron helped her during long drives and made them several hours shorter. I wasn't convinced but kept my mind wide open.

The next morning I was on my way to class. Since it was only the second month I lived in Scotland, I wasn't very familiar with the area and streets. I got to the city center an hour before the class and started to walk to the hotel where the class was held. I had walked for quite a while and arrived at the end of the street where I believed the hotel was. The scenery I saw was completely different. I had no idea what happened, as I was sure that I knew where to go. Luckily two policemen standing nearby helped me. Turns out I walked for half an hour in the wrong direction. It was an "L" shaped pedestrian street I started out right at the middle and walked in completely the wrong direction. I was told it would take an hour to walk to the hotel to get to my class.

Once I realized what happened, I started to run but after few steps I suddenly remembered about Metatron and time folding. "Great!" I thought, "This is an opportunity to give Metatron a job and put the tool I learned about in action to see for myself how it works." Still not being quite convinced that it would work, I did my visualization:

I imagined the color magenta around me and called Archangel Metatron in my mind: "Archangel Metatron, please fold time, please make sure I get to the class few minutes before the class starts!" Then, in my mind, I imagined a clock in front of me, drew a spiral anticlockwise, saw hands on the clock going backwards, took a deep breath in and out, thanked him for stopping time and making sure I got to the class in time. Then I walked to class in my regular "walking pace".

As I was already in the elevator in the hotel, I took out my cell phone to turn it off and was shocked to see the time. It was only 9:50am – 10 minutes before the beginning of the class which meant that what was supposed to be an hour's walk, I managed to make in about 20 minutes. Logically, there was no way it could have happened. I still was not quite convinced that it happened with the help of angels, but I sure knew that I tapped into some Universal energy that made it happen.

Interesting was the fact that several other students reported similar experiences that morning. Even though I wasn't yet convinced of angel existence I was much more interested. Then, it happened: I got my very first visible sign from angels.

Angel Feathers

I heard that one of the signs that angels indicate they are around is a feather. I didn't know if I believed it or not but kept my mind open to this idea.

I really loved colors and the idea of helping people by offering Color Readings. I was on my way home from downtown Glasgow – about 40 min. walk – and had the question on my mind: "how to make it happen, how to be able to afford to buy all the color bottles, where to start, what is the potential of me becoming full time Color Therapist..." Suddenly I felt chills all over my body and right in front of my eyes out of nowhere was a white feather floating in the air. I looked up and around – didn't see anyone or anything. Maybe it was a sign that ideas I was receiving answers to my thoughts and questions.

A few days later I had a similar experience. I was walking down the street and thinking about the "Colourworks" and working as a Color Therapist, which I was now qualified to do. Here it was again – a white feather right in front of my eyes out of nowhere and chills all over my body. More than once? It was too much to be a coincidence.

Around the same time my friend told me about Hay House Radio on internet, which I hadn't checked out, yet, but was going to as I felt something was there for me to hear. As I logged on, checked out all the shows that were offered and "Angel Therapy® with Dr Doreen Virtue" caught my attention. I saw that the host was the same woman whose Angels cards I already had. Of course I had to listen to this show. For the next few weeks all I listened to was Doreen's Radio program on the HayHouseRadio.com archives, some of them repeatedly.

My doubts about the existence of angels was greatly reduced, and by the time I had heard all the angel shows I believed angels were real. I would find feathers in the most unexpected places. At that time, I was working at a B&B where part of my responsibilities included cleaning rooms. I would turn off the vacuum cleaner, pull out the plug, and as I turned back around, I would find feathers right where I just cleaned.

I would also have many experiences of finding feathers in my room – on the bed, on the table, on the floor upon returning home as if the angels had a party while I was gone.

I also loved to talk about angels. There were times when the response from other people to my angelic talk was uniquely cute and fun. At the time I was taking voice lessons. I would find feathers on my way to lessons as well as in the room were lessons were held. Once, as I found a feather, I asked my voice teacher if she knew that when angels visit, they leave feathers. Her response was: "So do pillows!" ☺. Whether people believed in angels or not, I never got a response of not being accepted or my beliefs would not be accepted. After my childhood experiences, the feeling of acceptance I felt wherever I went that encouraged confidence in myself, my beliefs and my ability to share them with others. This was a major breakthrough in releasing my emotional blocks and becoming a healer and a Light worker. I was ready for what came next.

My Angel Visitation

One night soon after I was awakened by noises that sounded like whispering. I felt as if someone was next to me in bed and the energy was wonderful. Suddenly I "woke up" as I realized that nobody else human was there. I blinked my eyes few times to make sure I was awake. I called on Archangel Michael (I had learned through Doreen's radio program that he is the one that helps us to feel safe) to make sure I was safe and not harmed no matter what happens. I suddenly felt someone embracing me from behind and slowly becoming one with my body and me. It was such a weird feeling that I moved my hand a bit to make sure I still had control of my body. As soon as I moved I felt energy starting to leave my body and at that point I wanted to see what would come next. I told myself: "I am safe and all is well". As I did this, energy returned as one with me. I heard the whispering again. Suddenly I felt wings on my back. They were so much a part of me as anything else that I was used to in my body. Everything went silent and I felt myself fluttering my wings once then pausing for few moments, again fluttering and pausing. I was so taken by the experience I didn't dare move. Having wings amazed me yet I felt very safe. The whispering became louder. I was getting brave enough to slowly move my head towards the whispering noise. I saw something like a pathway and a crowd of angels. All were illuminated with light from inside and brightening the pathway that was filled with angels as far as I could see. Some of them were holding a light in their hands. All of them were looking at me as I looked at them. I felt amazing energy flowing through my body bringing a tremendous amount of joy, love and happiness that I wanted to last forever. I knew this angel visit was something rare and special. With that thought I fell asleep still feeling the wings on my back. The next morning I had the greatest feeling ever. I could see and feel the light within me and everyone. I felt as if I could fly (I had wings after all). I was encompassed with pure, unconditional love.

I knew with all my being that I was absolutely loved, no matter what I did or said. I felt safe and secure in this knowledge.

Having seen them and felt them, I was now certain about the existence of angels. With this incredible experience I also learned that even if we don't believe in angels, they believe in us. They are with us to help us and protect us at all times. This is their gift of complete and total love toward all of us.

Joining the "Angel Family"

I was very focused on working with "Colourworks" therapy and at that time I had no intention to work as an ANGEL THERAPIST® I didn't even know there was such a thing. The angels on other hand knew better.

Christmas was approaching and when I heard that a limited number of "Angel Guidance Boards" (like game board) by Doreen Virtue Ph.D. were available with her autograph, I ordered one for myself as a Christmas gift.

I received it a week before Christmas but decided to wait until Christmas to open it. That first night after receiving my gift, I saw Doreen in my dream. We passed by each other but didn't speak. As I woke up, I heard a voice say "Call her!" As I wondered what that meant I realized it was the day when Doreen's radio program was on Hay House Radio. I didn't have a computer at that time so there was no way I could listen to a live show but I could call and that was what I did. Magically, but not surprising, I got through the first time I dialed the number however the connection was lost so we didn't talk. I realized I had seen a premonition. I got through to Doreen's radio program, but we didn't speak just like in my dream.

On Christmas; I opened my gift and was absolutely taken by the energy of the "Angel Guidance Board". I felt connected to the angels more than ever before. The "Angel Guidance Board" had a different energy than the cards but it gave (still gives) perfectly correct answers and guidance just like cards. It wasn't until the beginning of the New Year that I had a dream with Doreen again, this time we talked and I woke up again hearing someone saying: "Call her!" I realized it was once again the day of Doreen's radio program. I still didn't have a computer, but I had the phone number and knew the time the show started.

I had no particular question to ask but I knew angels wanted me to call and I wasn't going to argue with them.

I did get through and felt chills and energy rush through my body. This time we got to talk – again, just like I had seen in my dream. The only one of Doreen's books I had read was "Goddesses and Angels". I was unaware of ANGEL THERAPY PRACTITIONER® Course. I admired her work from what I learned from listening to her radio program. I didn't know exactly why but after connecting to angels through Doreen on the radio, I decided to check out her website. There I spotted the ANGEL THERAPY PRACTITIONER ® course at the St. Regis Hotel in Dana Point, California. As I was reading the word "Regis", which seemed so similar to my name, I felt chills again all over my body and heard the angels urging me to go there. At the time I had no idea how it would happen and what it was about but I felt very strongly that angels wanted me to be in this class.

A couple of weeks after this message, my friend, who knew about the guidance I had received, sent me a message telling me to hurry and register for the ATP® course as she had heard there were only a few openings left.

I wondered how it would be possible for me to go to the USA, but the guidance I received was stronger than my doubts so I went to the bank. Living in the UK I had only a basic bank account and in order to pay for the class which had to be done upon applying, I had to transfer money to my home country's bank account which would enable me to pay over the internet. I had transferred money before for other reasons and the whole process took a couple of weeks but this time I needed it to happen fast. As I was on my way to the bank, I told my angels that if they wanted me to go to "their" course, they needed to help me to arrange for the money transfer immediately.

Amazingly, the money was transferred and in my other bank account by the next morning. Wow! The angels were in a hurry for me to register and move forward. A few minutes later I was a student of the upcoming ANGEL THERAPY PRACTITIONER® course.

After this, I felt like my angels were always guiding my life. Now that I was registered for the class, I didn't know how I would be able to get a visa for the trip to the USA. I was living in the UK and using my home country's passport, which limited eligibility for the most simple tourist visa. However, once again the guidance I received was strong enough for me to proceed.

In the meantime I made a dream board (for manifestation purposes: a dream board has photos, words and symbols of what we want in life, more about it in Chapter XI) on which I put the receipt for the ATP® course as an affirmation that the Universe would pay for my flight and the ATP® course (so I could use the money I already paid for the class to make my stay in USA few weeks longer), also affirming that I would get a visa to USA.

To make a long story short – initially I was refused a visa at the embassy and could hardly believe it since everything so far had felt "right" regarding me being in this class.

For a moment I started to doubt myself that I wasn't supposed to go after all, but that didn't feel right. I was told that the only reason I wouldn't receive a visa is there was not enough proof that I would return to the UK and that I didn't have enough attachment to the UK.

After my appointment at the embassy, I had 9 hours before my flight back from Ireland where the embassy was, to Scotland. I had lot of time to think and receive instructions from angels for the next steps to get me on my way to the USA.

As I walked downtown in tears of frustration and disappointment, I asked my angels to give me a sign of what to do. I suddenly stopped and looked up – **"FAITH"** is what I saw. I had stopped by a store called **"FAITH"**. I didn't feel like I could have much faith at this point, but again, it was pretty amazing how quick the angels responded.

After crying buckets of tears and much time walking around, I suddenly got a brilliant idea. The angels were especially pleased about me "getting the message" as they rewarded me with lots of angel bumps (like goose bumps).

The idea was to create a name for the healing services I offered and register it as a new business. As I got on the plane I made plans of what to call my business and what else I could do. My angels confirmed that I got it right by leaving some feathers on the floor right in front of me on the plane.

The very next day, I went to an agency office that my friend had advised me to go to a while back where anyone could apply for assistance in starting a new business. It offered individual support as well as specific classes and support meetings. As my visit to this agency was divinely guided it sure was quite a life-changing thing as well as miraculous. To make it as short as possible – I not only received help and advice in creating a new business, but my angels had arranged for this to be a way to pay for my flight and the ATP® course

It turned out that this particular agency was giving away a 1000 pounds (about $2300) grant as start up fund for people under 30 years of age who start a new business during the time of this grant offer. The timing couldn't have been more perfect for me. The grant I received covered fees for the class, the flight and hotel expenses.

I applied for a visa again. This time I was more prepared. In my application I mentioned how important it was for me to be in this ANGEL THERAPY PRACTITIONER® course, how angels are a big part of my life and how these are the best courses I knew, where to learn about angels. I also mentioned that this class is offered only in the USA.

The embassy questioned me in person about my angel business and the reason for my trip to the USA. Finally, I was told that even though they shouldn't be giving me visa, I would receive one to go to this class.

I was so happy and relieved! Now I could see why my visa application was refused initially. I had to go through this process of registering my business, as that's how the angels arranged for me to acquire the funds for this trip as well as the necessary requirement for coming back. This was the greatest lesson of how faith works – **we are given guidance, one step at the time. When we take notice and act upon it, we are then shown the next step. If something seemingly bad happens, it's important to remember to have faith as it's part of the plan and is leading us to what we have asked for, or something even better.**

Angels Join in Belly Dancing

This story starts a few months before me knowing about ANGEL THERAPY PRACTITIONER® course and coming to Laguna Beach, California to take it.

On a Hay House Radio program, I heard mention of a project that an artist in Laguna Beach, Gary Simpson, had been working on called "Commonground 191". His vision was to collect the soil or sand from each of the nations and incorporate the total mixture on a series of panels. Individual panels would reflect the identity of each nation representing the underlying unity. I learned that individuals and companies were invited to take part in this project by collecting and providing soil samples.

After visiting the website of this project I found out that soil from my home country was still needed. I volunteered to obtain it. This would have been the end of this story but my angels apparently had something more in store.

After I completed the ANGEL THERAPY PRACTITIONER® course I stayed in the area for another few weeks as part of my vacation. In Scotland where I lived at the time, I had started belly dancing classes and I was interested in trying out a belly dance class in Laguna Beach. As I walked around a local spiritual store, I asked if they knew any belly dance classes in the area and was directed to the message board filled with different business cards and promotions. Out of all the belly dance class ads one in particular got my attention. The class was being held that very same night and was close by. I got to the class early just to make sure I could get in. Luckily there was a space.

The class was filled with warm and loving energy. As far as I was concerned it was the best belly dance class and the best belly dance teacher ever – Jheri St. James. When Jheri found out I was originally from Latvia, she told me about her involvement in the art project by Gary

Simpson called "Commonground191". We were both surprised at this coincidence of our involvement in the same project.

We kept in touch after I returned to Scotland and about a year later when I returned for a Mediumship class, I was invited to meet Gary in his studio as well as to one of his "Commonground 191" exhibitions where the first series of panels were presented. This experience showed me the unexpected ways that angels show us where we are meant to be as well as who we are intended to meet on our journey.

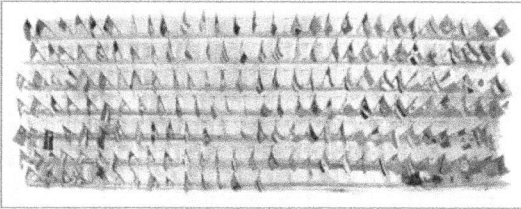

(wall with flags and soil from all over the world)

(commonground 191)

Mediumship and My Angels

As I was excitingly waiting for my trip to the ATP® course, I had lifelike dreams almost every night in relation to teaching. I was connecting to the teacher during my dreams, taking classes and teaching different classes. In my most significant dream I was in the class with 20 people and Doreen

Virtue was my teacher in this dream. I thought I was seeing the ANGEL THERAPY PRACTITIONER® course, but it turned out the class I signed up for had more than 20 people. During the ATP® course I found out that the same teacher was teaching a Mediumship class and it was limited to 20 students. This class was open only to certified ANGEL THERAPY PRACTITIONERS® and here it was again: proof that we are given guidance one step at a time. I had to go to the ATP® course in order to go to the Mediumship class. Of course the dream I was shown with me being in a class with 20 people did happen. Once again, I didn't have any idea what I was getting myself into. I never really understood why people would want to connect to deceased loved ones through others. I knew I could talk to my grandma who had passed if I wanted to, which I did from time to time, but it didn't occur to me that not everybody knew they could do it too. I never in my wildest and weirdest dreams thought I would be a channel between this world and the other side but the greatest thing I learned through this experience is **we don't need to know the how and the why, we just need to accept the guidance and have faith that it's taking us where we are meant to be**. The soul's journey is so rewarding and exciting, all of it: ups and downs, especially when we can look back and see how it all makes sense, see how all was perfect just the way it was, how the challenges had to be part of it. If things made sense in the past, why would that not continue in the present and future? I know for sure that we are always guided and it's our responsibility and choice to follow our intuition to be in alignment with the Divine plan for us (even if we don't know what exactly it is).

Earth Angels

Through the process of becoming and being part of the Angel Family through the ATP® course, I learned that there are people on this planet, who besides their own personal mission have another, more global mission. These are people who feel a strong responsibility toward others and want to be in service in some way. I learned that these caring people are called "Earth Angels". Doreen Virtue writes in her book: "Realms of the Earth Angels": "Divine spark of light is within everyone, however "Earth Angel's" spark of light has spent many lifetimes far away from Earth and those lifetimes have influenced who "Earth Angels" are today. According to where their soul has spent the most time, Earth Angels are "put" into different realms: Incarnated Angels, Incarnated Elementals, Starpeople, the Wise Ones, Blended Realms – Knights, Leprechauns,

Mystic Angels, Merpeople... (as time goes, many other realms are being rediscovered)".

This is when my love of all things magical, playful, childlike and serious at the same time made sense. Witches (Wise One Realm) and Fairies (Elemental realm) resonated with me the most.

Some of the qualities of Elemental Realm that described me - very shy and private even though they're extroverted, can't stand rules, do things because they want to and not because they must, love to be outdoors, protective of nature and animals, feel off center in the workday world, need time alone.

Wise Ones have friends whom they admire and friends who are "clients". They rarely have a chance to discuss their own troubles, intense individuals, like Elementals they dislike rules, are nervous about sharing their gifts as they remember the "Witch burning craze". Wise One would say: "I am different and proud of it!"

Learning this was a real breakthrough! I felt like I finally knew why I had felt so different my whole life. A lot of the events in my life made sense now and it helped me to really feel and know: "I am different and I proud of it!" I was able to accept and love my unique qualities. Also my experience that night with the angels and wings on my back now made sense. Finding out and realizing that all the experiences with angels that I was not so convinced about being real, have been very true and real, and that they have all been for a reason. They have enabled me to feel and know that I am "normal" just the way I am and my experiences were real. I am truly grateful for my angels as their unconditional love for me has replaced all the grief, trauma and pain I had in my life. Although I can recall my past painful experiences I now feel only love, understanding and peace.

Indigo Children

...During the time I discovered angels and connected with them, I also learned about the children of a higher degree of evolution than "normal" children who are said to have paranormal powers such as clairvoyance. I learned that these children are described as Indigo, Crystal and Rainbow getting their name according to the color of their aura – energy field around them. I learned that Indigos, in this ray of highly spiritual children, were born first and major wave of them were born in 1970's. Highly sensitive and psychic, having an important life's purpose, having a warrior spirit as their collective purpose is to revolutionize old systems that no longer serve us, highly sensitive to dishonesty "Indigo children", writes

101

Doreen Virtue in her book "Care and Feeding of Indigo children", "can sense dishonesty like a dog can sense fear. They know when they are being lied to or manipulated. Since Indigo children's collective life's purpose is to usher people into a new world of integrity their inner lie-detectors are needed.

The warrior spirit of Indigo children might feel threatening to some adults as well as the fact that these children are unable to conform to dysfunctional situations at home, work, or school. They also don't have the ability to dissociate from their feelings and pretend like everything's okay ...unless they are medicated or sedated."

In their book "The Indigo Children: The New Kids Have Arrived" authors Lee Carroll and Jan Tober write: 'Indigos respect the talents and abilities of each individual, but these talents do not make any one greater than anyone else. The play of ego and self-importance has no real place in the life of an Indigo"

During the Angel Therapy Practitioner's® course I also learned more about the Crystal Children as one of them was invited as a guest to our class. He was a boy with unique musical talent and played a Native American flute for us. It felt like his music touched my heart on the deepest level I had experienced. It is believed that Crystal Children are highly sensitive just like Indigo children, however their energy is calmer than the energy of Indigos as they are the peacemakers. Having extraordinary musical talent is one of the characteristics of Crystal children. After Indigo children have cleared the path with their warrior energy, Crystal children have come to bring the message of peace. They are here to make people happy, to help them get in touch with their true selves by awakening the connection deep within. You can read more about Crystal Children in "Crystal Children" by Doreen Virtue Ph.D. and "The Children of Now" by Meg Blackburn Losey, Msc.D., Ph.D. To me, the music of this particular Crystal child felt very angelic.

During the ATP® course mentioned above, I met many people who had felt different their whole lives, just like I did. Even though their experiences were different than mine, connecting with these people from all over the world helped me to appreciate all the experiences I had had. I wasn't alone, I wasn't the only one who had felt different. I had finally met others like me, not just one or two people but hundreds. Just like I resonated with some of the Earth Angel Realms I talked about in the previous paragraph, I deeply resonated with just about everything that I learned about the Indigo children.

As I was reading characteristics of an Indigo Child that Carroll and Tober define, my choice of my name made sense by the first characteristic mentioned: *"they come to the world of the feeling of royalty"*... I do believe that on a Soul level we choose our name before we are born. If our parents are good listeners, they hear the name and "give" it to us. If not, they give their children a different name. In most of the cases people who haven't gotten their "real" name, the name they chose on a Soul level, don't like their name and often change it in their adult years. Some of these people prefer to be called in nickname instead. My mom surely was a great listener as I love my name. How can I not: the meaning of my name, ReGina, is "the Queen". Back to one of the characteristics of an Indigo Child about the feeling of royalty – I had even chosen a royal name ☺!

Besides other spiritual characteristics that talk about Indigo children being extremely sensitive, telepathic, being vulnerable but powerful, having natural healing abilities, high sense of fairness, being wise beyond their years, creating and bringing in new ways of thinking and being for Planet Earth that made a sense of my early spiritual experiences, one that made the most sense regarding my feeling of "being different" and "not fitting in" is the following: *"They seem antisocial unless they are with their own kind. If there are no others of like consciousness around them, they often turn inward, feeling like no other human understands them. School is often extremely difficult for them socially"* (from *"The Indigo Children: The New Kids Have Arrived"* by Lee Carroll and Jan Tober).

Another one of Indigo children characteristics *"they are not shy in letting it be known what they need"* was extremely true as well. With the understanding I have now, when it comes to the challenges that my mom experienced with me, as I mentioned in earlier chapters, I believe was the fact that I would always tell what I like and what not. Even if she didn't listen, I had to "get it out", to "let it out". All the frustration that I had about the challenges in school and frustrating experiences outside, I couldn't hold in when I was at home. Even the smallest challenges at home would be enough to awaken all the frustration, disappointment and anger I had in life and would come out as shouting, slamming doors. *"Difficulty with discipline and authority, refuse to do certain things they are told to do, refuse to respond to guilt trips"* (for instance: my mom would often cry after we had had an argument but I felt, she is an adult but she doesn't hear me, doesn't understand me and I should be the one crying. I had no feeling of being guilty. All I felt was "it's not fair!"). These characteristics also fall into this category. Even if I wanted to do something, if somebody told me to do exactly that, especially if it was my mom, I wouldn't do it.

If nowhere else then at home, as much as possible, I wasn't going to let things happen the way other people wanted, I was going to have it all my way! Here is what Wendy H. Chapman (director of Metagifted Education

Resource Organization where she is enlightenment teacher of gifted children, indigo children and their families) defines as one of the characteristics of an Indigo child " Indigo children often express anger outwardly rather than inwardly and may have trouble with rage".

When it comes to Indigo children eyes that are said to be " very old, wise and deep looking" – I was always told even now as adult that I have unique looking eyes.

One of the other greatest challenges that in my adult years, now, I find to be actually fun, is the fact that Indigo children tend to *"reject the norm, tradition or what is expected by society"*. My belief is that there is no such thing as "right" or "wrong", "good" or "bad" therefore, as far as I am concerned, it's kind of hard to say what the "norm" is!

I found it to be very interesting that even though most of my childhood I wanted to feel like I belonged, wanted to fit in, now that my childhood's dream has come true and I have found where I perfectly fit in, I don't really need it anymore. I am perfectly fine with being who I am without fitting in anywhere else. Most important to me now is that I fit in with myself!

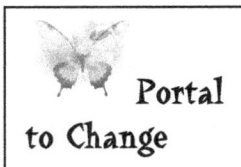

Portal to Change

What are your beliefs and experiences with angels, God, fairies, trust, faith? Were they mentioned in your family? Have you felt like the world was an unfriendly place no matter where you turned?

CHAPTER VI

Embracing My Uniqueness

"The things that make you an outsider in high school are the things that make you successful in life."

- Dr. Luayne Longfellow -

Some Lessons Learned

As I shared in previous chapters, I was pretty much living my life knowing that there was something different about me, more than just physical appearance, but without awareness of exactly what it was and without awareness that it's positive.

As long as I felt accepted, as I did with my activities in music, I loved to be different but in general, I was concerned about fitting in. By doing that, I would get tangled in seemingly endless circles of avoiding my own real self. With the great amount of limitations that seemed to be around, all I truly wanted was to be free.

I never really considered "who am I and what do I like?" but I knew what I didn't like as it seemed to be all around me. The more I focused on it, the more I experienced it. I somehow didn't put it together - if I can see negative, I also could see positive.

Being preoccupied with how to fit in, I rarely stopped to think of what I would like to do. Even though I did have dreams about my "perfect" world it still seemed unattainable once I got out of my dream state. With the understanding, knowledge and feelings I have now, I am grateful for having the experience of "trying to fit in" because it helped me to become aware that I am unique and no matter how I try, I can't be fake, I can't pretend to be who I am not, can't like what I don't like and I can't do what someone else wants if doesn't feel right to me.

Of course – there is no such thing as "can't" because anything is possible but when I say can't I mean to deny my awareness of who I am doesn't allow me to be my genuine self nor does it allow anyone else to be who they are not and feel happy and free.

I am grateful for all the experiences I had as I can say now, they taught me what I needed in terms of knowledge and understanding I have now.

Latvia, the country where I was born and grew up, is a magical place with so many green trees, flowers, plants, birds and animals, and fresh air, beauty in nature everywhere. I never thought I would ever appreciate it so much as I do now when I see how many blessings it has brought me. I appreciate the simplicity and gifts that nature has provided as part of everyday "normal" life. I give thanks for all the natural beauty that I used to take for granted.

From my early spiritual experiences I have learned to trust my inner guidance. I have learned that when I get the feeling of doing or not doing something, going or not going somewhere, saying or not saying something – it is Divine Guidance at work and I do not question it. Instead I just follow, take action (one step at the time) and trust that everything is happening for a reason, everything works out perfectly even if we experience challenges. I have also learned that challenges come into our lives to help us work out and let go of some old beliefs that are no longer serving us well and to evolve us into higher consciousness.

My own evolution, as I described, has reconnected me with the Spirit world of God, angels, fairies, dragons, unicorns and I learned how the healing power of thoughts and prayer can make dreams become a reality.

One of the greatest messages I have learned from the angels is the **importance of asking**. If we don't ask, we cannot receive answers or help. I have also learned that all requests are answered.

My experiences of being teased and bullied have caused me to take a look at my own wants and dreams and manifest them by using my inner resources such as focusing on my strengths and discovering that every problem can have a happy ending if we change our beliefs about the experience by changing our perception.

By loving and appreciating myself, I eventually learned that my passions can become a way to earn good money and it doesn't have to be as hard as it might seem, it's only a matter of perspective, how we choose to look at it and what we choose to believe. I have learned that each one of us has a free will to choose from countless opportunities and possibilities – we live in an abundant world and there is enough of everything for everyone, starting with choosing to think this way.

"I Wished You Were Normal"

I can't pin point a particular moment but most of my life I felt the expectation from my family, to be like someone else, to say something different, to act differently than I knew how.

I am lucky and grateful to have a family who is very open to all things spiritual. Recently my mom admitted to me that she didn't know what to do with me, how to raise me, how to be a mom to me as I was so weird. She shared that she compared me with other children and thought: "I wish ReGina were normal". It was the best thing ever that my mom could tell me, as that was the moment when it "clicked" for me and things made perfect sense. Like a flash, all the memories of "being expected to be someone else" came back and I finally knew what was behind it. Without being consciously aware of it, I had picked up my mom's thoughts and feelings, and from the moment it "clicked" this feeling was gone. It dissolved away as it was no longer needed. The time had come for me to know the truth and let go of the unspoken expectations I was carrying. This conversation with my mom was the most helpful as it seemed to lift an enormous burden off my shoulders and helped me close the chapter of "being who I am not" for good.

Even though they were not the most perfect family, I love them very much and I know they are perfect for me. The biggest lessons I have learned here have been **the importance of talking about feelings and anything that comes up, instead of making assumptions.** I have learned **the importance of accepting people for who they are instead of trying to change them**, gained the knowingness of how I want my family to be, learned the importance of appreciating small things and importance of helping others feel special yet equal at the same time.

No matter how much my mom wanted me to be "normal" I just couldn't. I have learned to live with and be proud of myself, and the way I am different! Proud to be different!

Proud to be Different

("car" for display in Latvia)
(I now take the driver's seat in my life ☺)

✦✦✿✦✦

I have come a long way in my soul's journey. I remember feeling stuck and wanting to die. I have become more aware and more alive than I can ever remember myself being. I am shouting to the world: "I am proud to be unique and different! I am proud to be who I am! I am enough just the way I am!"

My wish is for you to make the same choice to love who you are, to accept who you are without judgment, trust that you are safe. Have faith that only good and something better will result in this choice. Trust that you are who and where you are supposed to be right now.

When we are who we are all 100% - only something good can happen to us. Expect it and it will! As author Louise L. Hay affirms: "Only good lies before me!" And it does for you too.

Portal to Change

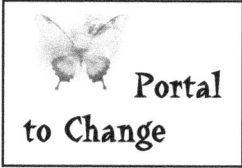

How do you feel in your life at the moment? Lonely? Sad? Happy? Confused? Neutral? Do you know and love how special and unique you are? Are you confident about yourself or do you doubt yourself and stop yourself from moving forward? What lessons have you learned from your most significant life's experiences?

✿ ✿ ✿

Affirmations I use to strengthen my love for my uniqueness and myself:

- *I love and approve of all aspects of myself.*

- *Life is good and all is well!*

- *I am in the flow of life!*

- *Abundance of all things positive flows in my life freely, easily and effortlessly!*

- *It's easy for me to be true to myself and express my truth to the world.*

- *When I express my true self, I attract only positive experiences in my life.*

- *It's safe for me to be my true self everywhere I go.*

- *I deserve all things positive.*

- *This World is a safe place to express my uniqueness.*

- *I love and I am loved unconditionally. I am loveable.*

- *I am ready to be powerful and unique right now!*

- *I am worthy to experience success in all I do!*

- *I am worthy to experience my dreams coming true!*

- *Every choice I make helps me to live my dream!*

- *It's safe for me to stand my ground.*

- *I love to be my unique self!*

- *It's safe and powerful to be my unique self!*

One way to use them: as you say these affirmations look into a mirror and hold your hand over your heart for further connection. Repeat them daily for as long as you can.

May you be your magnificent self
in touch with who you are
shining your Light brightly into the world!

- ReGina -

PART II

Embrace your Uniqueness

A Guide to Recognizing Our Uniqueness and Embracing It

The time we are living in now is so dynamic. It is the Age of Aquarius where so many of us are awakening, experiencing the need to help heal ourselves by looking within to discover who we are, what are the answers and what can we offer of ourselves to make a difference.

The idea about power of thought and law of attraction is circling the Globe, the value of following these ideas is shared by countless people, everywhere in the world, who have put them into action and experienced miracles happening.

It's amazing how many of us feel touched by seemingly simple things yet it's so powerful when we choose to listen and become aware.

"Our thoughts create our reality" and "the power of being present" seem to be the most heard messages that many claim to be the key for living the life of our dreams.

Living the life of our dreams is being free to be who we are in all aspects of our life, taking responsibility for our life in our hands, knowing that anything is possible and taking action.

The power of thought has been proved to be extremely powerful when it comes to creating our life. Thinking is something we all do, we often have "millions" of thoughts going through our mind at once. Just becoming aware of our thoughts, even if it is only one thought, brings more clarity in our life allowing us to make better choices, freeing us to be who we are, and living in a way that makes our heart sing.

It seems changes are happening around us more than ever before. The truth is – they have always been here as change is a law of nature. Now more of us are choosing to become aware of this change, aware of the possibility to make changes and the positive opportunities that they bring. The importance of taking responsibility for our life instead of blaming others, importance of honoring our true feelings, trusting the guidance we get, and taking action... it all somehow leads us towards being who we are. Throughout history this has been experienced by everyone everywhere: as time goes – what was good in the past has to be released to make a space for new. Different beliefs and ideas dominate at different times. This is the time when we are asked to get to the bottom of our truth, get in touch with ourselves on the deepest level and live from this space.

As we become more aware of who we are, what we have come here to be and do, we get in touch with the deepest level of ourselves. This involves all aspects of our life and being: our body, our emotions, our relationships and any situation we are experiencing. When we are not in touch with who we are, our spiritual and physical bodies are not in alignment and it can be easy to get confused and sidetracked. The more we learn about ourselves our bodies, spiritual and physical, become more aligned and we become less and less confused. It's very much related to being present. We can look at it this way: we have our physical body which is present wherever we go, but if our mind travels, we have "millions" of thoughts at once – our spiritual body splits into tiny pieces and goes in different directions... if we look through all these million pieces with our eyes (physical or inner) all we can see is a blur. If we are present then there is no blur since our physical body and mind are both here, they are in alignment.

The same applies to each one of us being different: there are no two things the same on this planet and we are not an exception. What does "different" mean? It means not the same, unusual. I believe that saying "no two snowflakes are the same" can be applied to anything and anyone.

Every one of us is unique and even if we wanted to, there is nothing we can do to change it. If we try to be someone else, part of us comes out of alignment, if we are saying something just to say it, but it doesn't come from our heart, part of us comes out of alignment again and it creates chaos and confusion in our mind, body and soul.

Love is the purest form of energy and exists in every living being. In our human body, love is related to the heart. Often our ideas and actions seem to be "born" in our mind and head but ideally they would be born in our heart. When it comes to love and heart: heart represents this love within us. When we are in alignment with who we are, there is also no confusion in our heart. All we do and say comes from a place of love in our heart. When we can't follow, what we do contains less love and other, lower vibrating energies.

For many years, most people have believed that something bad is going to happen if they allow others to see them for who they are. A lot of anxiety has resulted around fear of not being accepted, fear of rejection, fear of being alone, fear of losing friends, fear of losing jobs...we could make a long list here, but is it worth it? All the fear has created confusion where many people are in jobs that they don't like, are surrounded by people and situations that they don't like, act based on outside influences and later regretting it, and so on...

Things are always changing and the time we are living in now, is extremely dynamic as consciousness is being brought to awaken the soul and spirit, changing the way we see the world and ourselves to allow into our life whatever makes our heart sing. As we evolve we creates changes around us that are always for the better.

Whether we are aware of it or not, everything and everyone in this life is connected. We are all from the One Source. Friendships are one of the relationships that bring our consciousness of connection to the higher state. On a soul level we are all connected but on a physical level, we don't always feel this connection. Having real friends is one of the actual proofs of connection in the physical realm.

Friends are people that we feel connected to sometimes without knowing why. We share similar interests, beliefs and our time together brings us fulfillment. Having friends helps us to feel like we belong, helps us to feel connected. The more time and energy we invest in our friendships, the more meaningful they become.

A real friendship gives us the feeling of acceptance, unconditional love, joy, feeling that somebody cares, a feeling of being wanted. Every time we connect with friends, it deepens our relationship, we learn more about each other, we have more to share and a deeper sense of connection is developed.

What this part of the book focuses on is our friendship with ourselves. In order to be able to embrace our uniqueness, becoming friends with ourselves is essential. Any healthy friendship creates feeling of fulfillment and connectedness, and those feelings are necessary for us to have for ourselves if we are willing to embrace our uniqueness.

The most important part of life is not what we read in books, what we hear from others, it's our experiences. One way or another we are all connected, but our world starts within us. Only through our own experience a deeper sense of everything related to this experience is developed. For instance, only when we have experienced love within and all related to it, we can share it with others, only when we have experienced acceptance within by accepting ourselves, we can accept others. We must be as kind and loving to ourselves as we are to our friends

When it comes to the power of being who we are and embracing our uniqueness, the most important requirement is to become friends with ourselves, to develop a sense of connection with ourselves. Just like it is with every friendship on a physical level, healthy friendships require investing time and energy into developing them, the same with becoming friends with ourselves. In order to develop relationship with ourselves it's necessary to invest time and energy into this relationship. The quality of our relationship and our sense of who we are depends on the time and energy we invest into being friends with ourselves.

The following part of the book offers insights on different aspects of our uniqueness with the intention of helping you to become friends with yourself and who you are. They are created to guide you toward remembering your true essence, strengthening it and proudly embracing your uniqueness. I share knowledge gained from lessons I've learned on my journey of embracing my uniqueness along with knowledge and messages received from the Spirit world on this topic (shown in Italic). This part of the book also offers different exercises that help in the journey of embracing one's uniqueness.

There is no better time than NOW.

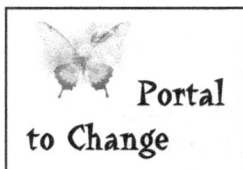

Portal to Change

When we think of something we open up a portal from our center to whatever it is we think about. What is on another side is free to come in. <u>Keep in mind that whenever you do exercises in this book you are opening a portal.</u> Things are going to change exactly at a perfect speed and timing, no more or less as you are ready for changes!

CHAPTER VII

We are Meant to Be Different

If all of us are thinking the same then somebody is not thinking as we are all meant to be different.
- Author unknown -

Being different means being not alike in character or quality; it means being not identical.

Everything and everyone is unique, but we don't become unique and different by adapting uniqueness to who we are, we are different by being who we are, by being in touch with our true essence and allowing this uniqueness to blossom.

First of all our soul comes to this Planet with different backgrounds, different experiences, it is born in a different time, different place, born to different parents, surrounded by different people, different situations, different circumstances and this list could be endless.

Every one of us is part of the human family – in a way we are One as unique beings at the same time we are part of Universal Oneness: we are One with all that there is. Each one of us has different talents and gifts, each one of us is good at something, each one of us has at least one dream that's different from others.

Just like no two snowflakes are alike, we are not like anyone else. We are the only ones who have the exact combination of all the ingredients that define our potential, our uniqueness. Everyone of us has at least one, usually more, uncommon skills that we are good at. Of course – there might be other people good at this one thing too, but when we add the other ingredients of ourselves to our talent and others add theirs everyone becomes unique being.

Because life, living and being alive has many aspects, different souls are needed to represent these aspects. Each living being therefore is different in many ways depending on which role they are filling. Because everyone has a soul that lives within, every one of us knows what's best for us.

Our true self is our Soul in its deepest level. When we can live our life loving ourselves, others and life with all it's *"connections" (more about "connections" in following chapters)* without being influenced by them in a destructive way, when we can have awareness and clarity about any aspect of our life and we act upon it, we are true to ourselves and are shining our light to the world.

Loving Ourselves, Others and Life

What do we understand as "love"? Love is the highest energy created, it is a feeling of strong liking for someone or something, it is profoundly tender and passionate affection for oneself, others or a situation.

Often we think that love only comes with romance and romantic relationships, but it is only one aspect of love.

To love ourselves means to feel connectedness of all that is and feel the Universe within. It is like a warm feeling inside our whole being where we know that all is well, we are safe and loved, it is when we do what makes us feel good in all aspects of life, when we don't try to prove or judge anything or anyone, when we see the Light and love within every being, it's where we can just be.

Loving oneself is an art on it's own. We don't always love from our hearts, we love, or think that we love but it comes from our mind. However true love for others is possible only if we love from inside.

Louise's L. Hay work and her idea of "mirror work" is extremely helpful when it comes to loving ourselves. The main idea is: you look in the mirror and say to yourself "I love you, (your name). I really, really love you!" My experience shows, when you can do that and feel the words and feeling behind it resonate on all levels of your being – then you have come to the point where you truly love yourself.

This is what spirit realm had to say: *"One very common thing that we see you doing is – believing that, when you try to please others, you show that you love them. That's not really the energy of love rather than feeding your ego. On the soul level, it is impossible to lie as our soul can see the truth no matter what. When you act from mind space instead of love, you often do great things for others that make you feel good, but there is no feeling of love behind it and on a soul level the other person can feel it too. There you can see that you have satisfied your ego, but it's not truly helping others. It's you caring for the "good feeling" instead of being love. This is also the case where you can feel not appreciated, where you feel like it wasn't worth it, where you feel sorry for yourself: "I am doing this for you, but this is what I get back! You don't care!" This is also a case of you trying to help by doing what you think is best for the other person rather than allowing others to let you know what is the help they need.*

Remember – there is more than one truth and what's right for you might not be right for the person next to you. Imagine – you really, really want someone just to listen, no judgments, no advice, just listen but instead you are being told what to do or worse, what you have done wrong and what you should do... Do you feel good receiving what you didn't ask for? Do you feel like you have received help in your situation? Do you feel fulfilled and it has helped you to move forward?"

It is impossible to lie to ourselves. If we do not receive what we are looking for on the soul level, even with good intentions the outcome is not so good. We might even feel frustrated and annoyed by what the other person has been saying. Our mind might not be aware that it's not what we asked for, but our soul knows – "all I want and need is for someone to listen – no judgments, no advice". And we walk away looking for what we need somewhere else.

This leads to another important point in this topic that is listening. When we do love ourselves we listen to our body, we listen to our emotions and feelings, we listen to our intuition. Every one of us knows about ourselves the best, we know what is it that we need no matter what situation it is. If we love ourselves we listen and hear the answers, we hear the guidance and then we can act. If we love ourselves, we know how to listen, we hear the messages that help us in situation we are in. It's the same when it comes to loving others. When we love ourselves and know how to listen, it's easier for us to listen and hear the messages for others and hear the best possible way to help another person. This way we do end up actually helping them, not annoying (if we help others when they are not ready or willing to receive help, it's easy to annoy them).

Spirit Realm says: *"When you do love yourself, you accept yourself for who you are no matter what it would be. You know that you are the best you that there is, you are doing the best you can in any situation and you know that so are the other people. Every one of you is doing your best in the situation you are in. When you can see that, you can accept others and all they do on the highest level possible. Why do you wear the clothes you wear? Why do you choose the words you say? Why do you act the way you do? Isn't it because you believe it to be the best way to be, act and handle the situation? Every one else is doing the same – they are living the best way possible from their understanding. Because everyone is different – everyone's best is different too."*

We can expect for another person to act the way we would have acted, talk the way we would have talked, but this expectation is never met. When we can see and accept the fact that all of us are different and therefore all we do is different and unique from anyone else's doing, we have come to the space of unconditional love: loving ourselves and others.

When we are in a place where we accept and love ourselves – the very natural process is to love our life as well, to love all aspects of it.

This is what Spirit Realm wanted to add: *"We see it as fulfillment. It's like this – when you love yourself you are fulfilled, there is nothing more to be done in order to feel the love, it's there. The truth is – it's always there, but not all of you see or feel it but when you do, it gives you the feeling of being fulfilled. On the deepest level of your soul, your life has a meaning and you can feel it.*

Now, you all seem to know that there has to be some meaning for your life, otherwise what's the point of living. When you actually feel it, everything falls into place. (We will give you some tools to help you get there later.) Imagine you have a math problem to resolve – when you don't know how to resolve it nothing makes sense, you don't see the meaning of the numbers but once you learn how to solve it, suddenly it all makes sense. The same is with the meaning of life – once you see and accept that everyone and everything has it's own purpose, and they are part of a bigger picture, everything makes sense and gives fulfillment. Every step in the process of being is fulfilled and filled with love."

Signs of Being in Touch With Our Uniqueness and Loving Ourselves

Just the way everyone is different, everyone might experience their uniqueness differently, however there are some key guidelines.

When we really, really want something and sooner or later we get it, imagine how great we feel when we get what we want? It's a positive feeling, isn't it? I like to say: " It makes our heart sing."

Now if we think how it makes us feel when we don't get what we want, things don't go the way we want them to go. Is it a positive feeling or is it more negative?

That's how we can tell if we are in touch with our uniqueness or not. On the Soul level every one of us knows who we are, what we are here for, what we are meant to do, what's our life purpose. We see and know the bigger picture, we know life to be the one having endless possibilities and opportunities. Life and living makes our heart sing, we see Light within

120

each one and everything, we see opportunities everywhere, we know life to be filled with fun and joy, we know it to be enjoyable – every aspect of it. We know how to trust and have faith as we are always given as much knowledge and tools for us to be able to do what we are meant to do, we hear the guidance we receive and act upon it without questioning, we experience miracles every step on the way.

Once our souls are in a human body it's easy to forget all the above, store it deep inside where the conscious mind doesn't go very often. When that happens we start to feel like life is a struggle; everything seems to go wrong, we see bad things happening around, we become angry with ourselves, others and life, world seems crazy, we feel exhausted, stressed, have challenging time to sleep and nothing seems to be going right.

It's simple as this **- when we are in touch with our uniqueness, life seems to be a happy place no matter what happens. We see opportunities everywhere; we see everyone and everything equally valuable, we see challenges as opportunity to grow, lesson to be learned. We see the other people as unique and honor them for who they are, we love ourselves for who we are and feel it on the deepest level of our being, we live our life and mean every thought we think, every word we say, every action we take. We also do work that is meaningful and we are proud to be who we are.**

To put it all in few words – we live a meaningful life and are consciously aware of all that there is.

If we are not in touch with our uniqueness and who we are, we go through life relying on outside sources such as: other people, TV, Radio, co-workers, boss at work, friends, family, teachers, priests, books... and others. Please do get it the way I mean it – I am not saying all the mentioned outside sources are bad, I mean - if we make choices based on what these sources tell us without asking ourselves "Does it feel right for me? Does it feel good for me to do?" that's when we are not in touch with our true self.

It's interesting how fear has been the major cause of people relying on outside source. On the deepest part of our being – we as souls do know that love is all there is, we are safe no matter what happens. Being in a human body during this lifetime, for one reason or another, has made many of us forget about this fact.

| Portal to Change

Getting in Touch With Who You Are

Here are questions to consider that help you recognize if you are in touch with who you are (you may even want to write them down). Read the question several times to allow yourself to hear it.

Do I know what makes my heart sing and what is it? – partner, job, family, financial situation, emotions, feelings, *physical activities, food... etc

Do I do/practice what makes my heart sing? How do I do it?

✿ Do I know what my strengths are and my weaknesses? What are they?

STRENGHTS   WEAKNESSES

✿ Do I focus more on my strengths rather than weaknesses?

✿ How I feel about different aspects of my life (family, work, finances, health…)?

Do I stick to my beliefs and stand my ground? When I do it and when I don't?

Do I feel good and positive about myself, what I do and my life? If not, what is it that I would like to improve?

Do I see problems and challenges as opportunities to grow? Name some examples!

Honoring our true feelings means we know what exactly we feel about any particular situation. Do I honor my true feelings?

SITUATIONS WHERE

I HONOR MY TRUE FEELINGS   I DON'T HONOR MY TRUE FEELINGS

Do I stay true to myself and my beliefs no matter where I go and who I talk to?

What are the situations I stay true to myself and what are the situations I don't stay true to myself?

TRUE   NOT TRUE

🦋   Do I feel confident about who I am and what I have to say?

🦋   Do I love my body and honor it? What do I do to honor my body?

🦋   Do I see other people as friends or as enemies and why?

Do I let other people be who they are or do I have the need to fix them? Why do I feel the way I feel?

Do I feel responsible for my life and what happens to me?

Do I blame others for what happens in my life?

What are the situations where I feel responsible for my life and what are the situations where I blame others? Name some examples!

Do I trust my intuition, gut feelings and act upon them?

Name some examples of the most significant experiences where you trusted your intuitions, acted upon it!

Do I know my talents and gifts? What are they?

🦋 Do I express my talents and gifts in my life?

Write down your answers as it helps to see things more clearly for what they are and you might even find connection between them.

The more positive your answers to these "power thought" questions, the more in touch you are with your own uniqueness.

Trust and Faith

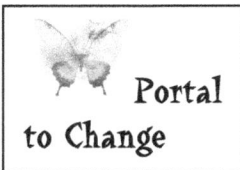

Just by choosing this experience of being born in a human body, we have chosen to have the lesson of trust and lesson of faith. What is trust and faith? The best way to describe trust would be a confident expectation of something to happen, a feeling of security. Faith is a belief that is not based on proof, confident belief in the truth, value, or trustworthiness of a person, idea, or thing. It is important to remember that on the soul level we all know how to trust and how to have faith, we know that everything happens for a reason, we know that it's important to trust the inner guidance we receive and take action even if it seems to make no sense. When we are in this physical body, our mind tends to forget that. And then comes the next lesson – the importance of learning to balance mind and spirit.

They all take a great part in us embracing our uniqueness as often we might need to have trust and faith that it's ok to be unique, it's safe to express ourselves, to follow our guidance even though it might not make sense, even though we might be misunderstood... trust and faith is very much needed to have for us to walk our talk. Since we are unique, our true self will differ from others and the collective "norm" which might bring up some fear and doubt. Strong trust and faith helps us to go through it with ease.

Trust and Faith

🦋 **Portal to Change**

Imagine a vertical scale where the lowest point is on the bottom and highest (complete trust and faith in this case) on top. When it comes to you having faith and trust, where do yourself being on this scale? Closer to the top, closer to the bottom, in the middle? Remember, we are all different and no matter where you find it to be – it's all good and great!

🦋   Think of some situation in your life where you were guided to do something, you trusted the guidance, followed it through and outcome was greater that you thought it would be, greater than you could have imagined.
(examples that I have found to be the greatest example for trust and faith, also the most simple ones:
*getting the feeling to call someone and few moments later receiving a call from this person.
*feeling like taking umbrella with me on a sunny day - few hours later it starts to rain)

🦋   Now – bring back the memory of you trusting something and the rewards it brought (keep in mind – all great things are simple: it can be the most simple thing). Visualize it as clearly and strongly as you can.

🦋   Then think of situation in you present life where you feel like you could use some trust and faith (it can be any situation).

Close your eyes and imagine the challenging situation in your present life that you would like to receive the guidance, as clearly as you can. Then ask in your mind "What is the next step for me in this situation?" "What is the best thing for me to do in this situation?". Listen for the answer as it can come in many different ways – as an image, as a thought, as a smell, as a sound, as an idea...

Now visualize yourself following the guidance you just got.
(notice if it makes you feel great or if it makes you feel not so great. Now you can use one of the tools (shared below) to change it.)

Go back to the memory of the time in your past where you trusted the guidance and outcome was unexpectedly positive, remember how it felt and then switch the situations – keep the positive, trusting feeling but this time with the situation in your present life. Visualize yourself following the guidance and keep the positive feeling seeing yourself receiving your gifts.

Keep in mind – if you trusted once and outcome was good, it can happen again and again, and in this situation too.

As soon as you catch yourself experiencing fear of trusting and having faith – remember the most positive situation where your trust and faith was richly rewarded. Bring this feeling into a situation where you feel fear and see how much easier it is to trust.

After practicing this exercise several times – check the scale mentioned at the beginning of this exercise
and see where your trust and faith level is now.

CHAPTER VIII

Awakening Our True Self

Knowing Our True Self

The most important thing in becoming aware of our true self and embracing our uniqueness is to develop a great relationship with our true self.

The Spirit Realm says: *"To know what we are talking about when it comes to our true self, first we want to clarify, make it easy to understand what we mean.*

Imagine your beautiful Soul as a ball of light that is inside your physical body.

The most pure form of who you are is your Soul. Then your Soul is born into a physical body. Time goes by and with every experience you have, there are connections created with all you have come in contact with. Once you have come in contact with something, the path has been created for you to go back and forth.

Imagine – let's say you are snowed in and in order to go somewhere, you need to take a shovel and make a path. As soon as way is made, you can use it to go back and forth if you choose so."

Our Web" Connections

The whole Universe is like one big web (imagine multidimensional spider web).

We are all connected on one level or another – directly and indirectly. Directly we are connected to people when we

Life's Web

know them personally, emotions we experience for ourselves, situations we are in, <u>indirectly</u>, when we don't know people, haven't experienced situation or certain emotion, don't resonate with it. However there is always somebody or something we resonate with that resonates to other person who resonates with a person or situation that we don't and that way we are still connected only indirectly.

Differently form Spider web, there is no one center in Life's web. Every connection place/point in Life's web is the center to some other web. Each connection creates/ invokes different emotions, is related to different emotions.

When it comes to our individual Life's web center, ideally we have a strong center of the web as that is us who we are. When we have embraced our uniqueness, we are in balance, we are in our power and all of our energy is centered. We acknowledge ourselves for who we are, we know ourselves, we are aware. We express ourselves and our talents fully, we feel safe to be who we are. We are connected to others, there are threads connected to the middle of our web's center, but they don't have power over us. We see where threads come from, are connected and just by being ourselves, in ideal case, we are avoiding these connections to influence us in a negative way. It is our choice how our life's web looks. Similar to a choice on the computer: We can choose to write in "**bold**" letters or "regular". The ideal Life's web center is "written" in **bold** (**bold** representing us being fully who we are, being in our power) and threads in regular. If we choose to feed on threads, no matter what they might connect us to, these threads turn from regular to "**bold**".

We do want to have many threads, many connections but leave them regular, not "**bold**". When our Life's web center is in "**bold**", it is a positive thing, high vibrating energy when threads that connect us to outside turn "**bold**" it's indication that we have given our power to outside source and it turns negative – lower vibrating energy.

*The color of Life's web is gold – the color of inner power, color of alchemy, color of royalty. Especially shiny the gold is at the center of each one of our individual web. Gold represents and is the spark of light that is within us. When we allow threads to attach and give our power away, more "**bold**" threads in our web are born and less energy that is "**bold**" is left for our Life's web center. We have given our power away and when we become aware of it we can choose to claim it back!*

<u>Let's look at this idea:</u>

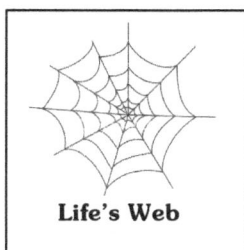

We are in the middle of the web and every time we get in touch with something or someone – new thread is created. It is now like a road to all our experiences of all the people we have been in contact with, all the emotions, all the experiences and all situations. Once we have experienced something it's part of us – so the path is created and now it's up to us, how much time and energy we want to invest going down this road. The more we walk down the road, the more we connect with the energy of it. It also depends how much we are connected with people involved. Most of the threads (in the "spider web" example) and roads are connected to the closest people, i.e., family, friends. Just like we are connected to different people in our life and have these threads between us, others have their own "spider" network, which we are automatically connected to once we begin contact with other people. Threads also connect with each other depending on how much the experiences are related among themselves.

Life's Web

Also we can get very much affected by all our experiences, all the situations and people on our path. The bigger our 'spider network" gets, the easier it can be to get lost in all the threads created and stay centered, stay in our power. It can be very easy to forget about our true self and get caught up in one or more places in the web.

The important thing is to remember that we are always connected to the Source, to all that is as it strengthens who we are and helps us to shine our light the very core of our being.

There is a powerful energy of light in the Universe. It is mostly referred to as God, Source, Universe, Creator. No matter what this Light is called, it's there. Imagine that every time a child is born, a part of this Universal Light is placed into the physical body. This is our connection to the Highest energy that there is and since it lives inside us, it's always there.

Just like there are many stars and planets in the sky and each one of them is different, just like snowflakes that appear the same yet each one of them is different, just like places on this Planet – they are all on Earth, but so different, the same way it is with the Soul: it comes from one Source yet each one of them is different, each one of them is equally valuable, each one of them connected.

Because life has many aspects, different Souls are needed to present these aspects. Each living being therefore fills a role in this life they are filling. Because everyone has a soul that lives within this physical body, everyone of us knows what is the best for us, it's just the matter of being still, and listening to our inner voice.

Being Aware

"People first need to realize and accept that they are unique. Acceptance is not always the easiest thing, but it's important as you move forward to this golden age –a time that offers so many great opportunities to grow individually and as a group. There is a great need to stay centered in your whole being, centered in your truth to be able to tap into the energy of golden wisdom. What is this golden wisdom we are talking about you might wonder? It's you, each one of you as you embrace your uniqueness. There is no time to lose by doing meaningless things that don't bring joy in your life and NOW is the perfect time to embrace this truth. You see, each generation has different lessons to learn as a group and individually. You have come, now, to the point in your life, where this collective lesson to learn is – to be who you are and have a blast being your true self.

We have been watching you from above and have been extremely delighted to see the shifts that are happening and how they are happening. If you would watch the Planet from above you would see how energies are moving, how there would be darker spots and lighter, and you would be surprised to see how quickly and easily light takes over any darkness that's still left. Please understand it right – dark doesn't certainly mean – bad, it simply means that energy there has been lower than Light.

Here we want to talk about the lower and higher energies. We see everything as the energy – physically touchable things and not touchable, all is energy and everything is vibrating on a different level. Once you have connected with something that is resonating on the same level as you are – one aspect of you or other - it makes this particular energy to grow and expand.

So here is what is important to understand about lower and higher energies – anything that creates any kind of negative feelings in you or in others, is vibrating on a lower energy level, all that is creating positive feelings in you or other's is vibrating on a higher level. It's also about messages that you are giving and receiving – if the message is positively encouraging, it is vibrating high, if the message is discouraging, uses negative words – it's vibrating on a low level. All of the energies are great as they serve a purpose, however the true essence of all the living things and the Universe is love and love is the highest vibrating energy that there is.

We talked about being in alignment with our spiritual and physical self in a previous chapter, it's just like that with the Universe – the more of you are vibrating on this highest energy - the more you are in alignment with the Universe, as a group and individually.

The dark and light spots, we mentioned earlier are this lower and higher vibrating energy, darker being lower and lighter being higher. What we are seeing happen now is – it's getting lighter in record speed. You see, when you are in alignment with who you are, even when you have these different thoughts cross your mind: "What am I doing? Do I like what I am doing in my life? Am I being true to myself? Wait a minute, this is not who I really am! What is the truth? What is life all about? What is the meaning of life? Do I love my job? Do I love to connect with people I am surrounded with? How can I change my life?" and similar thought along these lines... these kind of thoughts are raising your vibration already, even more when you talk about it and take action to change."

When we become consciously aware of life and different aspects of it, we have tapped into love and truth that is within us, we have tapped into knowingness, into higher realms than before and that's when the awakening of the soul is happening.

When we just go along with life and live unconsciously, we feel like things are happening to us, we might even feel like victims, we feel unhappy about our life, we feel the need to blame others in our unhappiness and we aren't even aware of our unconsciousness.

Awareness is when we start to see the bigger picture behind all that is happening within us and around us.

If we look at ourselves as spirit having a physical body, our spiritual and physical bodies starts becoming aligned as soon as we become aware, even when it is the awareness of being not aware. Aware is just the same as knowing. We may have heard people say: "The more I learn the more I realize that there is even more to learn." That's one example of being aware - even knowing that you don't know is being aware rather than claiming that we know everything, which would be a clear example of not being aware.

If you are reading this book you are already aware on one level or another, however, if you do feel you want to increase your awareness about life in general or any specific situation – here are some simple and effective things you can do as part of your daily spiritual practice:

1. Affirmations

You can say them throughout the day as many times as you feel guided, you can write them on a little piece of paper and stick on some place that you pass by often during the day – every time you look at it, read it. Affirmations guarantee success.

"I am aware"

"I am willing to be aware"

(in case it doesn't feel right, if we feel like it's not true yet, this affirmation shows the Universe our willingness to be aware and allows the shift to happen easier).

"I allow myself to be aware"

(often we feel like this is what we want, but when it comes – we don't allow it in due to fear)

2. Meditation

All you need for meditation is the willingness to go to a quiet and a quite place (even if it is a bathroom, when you feel you need some clarity in situation when you are at work, or having a stressful situation at home, a bathroom is the one place, where you can go and have some moments of privacy) and a few minutes time (meditation can be as short or as long as you wish it to be).

Take few deep breaths, belly breaths as I call them, where we breath in our belly feeling it expand as we breathe in, without the shoulders going up and down, then every time we breathe in, we think "aware" or "I am aware", every time we breathe out – think "I am aware".

3. Prayer

Dear, (God, Universe, Jesus, Spirit... ask whoever you believe in), I need your help. I am willing to be aware and increase my awareness in all aspects of life. Please help me to release any blockages that there might be in my awareness, in all directions of time, right now. Please make sure that with every breath I take, my awareness increases and it brings

138

blessings to me and everyone else involved. I ask for this or something better. Thank you

4. Affirmative prayer

Thank you, God (again, address the prayer to who ever you believe in and are asking for help) for helping me to increase my awareness. Thank you for making sure I am aware at all times in all situations. Thank you for removing any blockages from my being aware. I am grateful for my increased awareness.
And so it is.

Awareness starts with just one choice from us, choice to be aware, choice to become aware, our willingness to see the bigger picture, to see the truth. When it comes to truth, it is important to remember that there is more than one truth. When we can see and accept that, we have already become more aware than before.

It's all about the vibration we are resonating with.

... Spirit Realm says: *"When you are aware, you are seeing situations accurately, you are seeing that your differences are just differences, not subject to proving your truth to be the only truth there is, not subject to anger or resentment. When you are aware, you see how there is a connection between different people, how different people attract different situations, how they are attracted to different things. And when you look deeper then you see that all of the people who are involved in certain situations are having something in common, in other words – more or less they are vibrating on the same level. "It's almost like there are many worlds around us and based on vibration we are in, we have chosen one to live in."*

"The most important thing in becoming and being aware is – to become aware of who you are and how we are in different aspects of life. Once you start to become aware of you, who you are, you start to notice and see others for who they are, everything for what it is in the bigger picture of life."

Talents

Anything is possible whether we believe it or not. With practice we all have an ability to learn any skill however each one of us is born with a special natural ability. Talent is something that we are good at without any effort to be good at it. Each one of us is born with at least one talent (usually we have more than just one talent).

Life's Web

We are in the middle of the web when we are in our power. That is also the place where we own our talents and express them as we don't know any different. The older we get, the more we get in contact with other people, situations, we have more experiences. Depending on people and situations around us, we might start to forget who our "true self" is and choose to learn and achieve something that outside sources – parents, family, friends, society, government want rather than developing and using our own inner source. The more we focus on what someone else is good at (even wanting to be like someone else) the more threads in our web are being created going outwards. The more energy we put into these outside sources, the more of our power we give away. When we give our power away it weakens our own unique talents as there is less and less energy flowing there. Everything and everyone needs energy to live!

Here it is again our choice – do we choose to invest our energy into outside talents or our own?

One of the most asked question is: "What is my life's purpose? What is my life's mission?" The answer is extremely simple. Our life's purpose, life's mission is being ourselves and living our truth. However living it can be the most challenging thing ever. It's being aware, doing something we love to do and are good at. It all vibrates at a high energy level therefore by living our passion, our talent we are attracting only high vibrating energies - situations, people, and experiences. Our talents are like pointers, guidance from within that shows us what we have come here to do.

If we choose to live a free and meaningful life, be joyful and love our

140

life, we follow our inner guidance; we use our talents to fulfill our mission, to live our purpose.

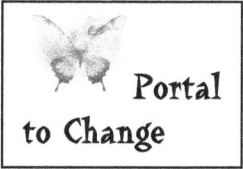

Becoming Friends With Your Talents

Portal to Change

Write down a list of all the things you know and feel you are good at, all the things you have talent and enjoy.

(imagine that you are looking at yourself with the eyes of God – how would God see you?)

Have your talents helped you in some way in your life? How?

Do you believe your talents can help your dreams come true?

Life is changing all the time, we are changing, everything around us changes. Have you noticed how you see different things and situations differently from how you saw them before?

Portal to Change

Things Change When We Change

Look back at your childhood: what were the most important things for you in your life then? What do you focus on the most now? How has your main focus changed?

❧ Pick a situation or an issue from the past where your believes about this situation have changed. How have your believes about it changed?

❧ What do you believe to be reason for this change?

❧ Pick one area of your life, one belief, one situation, one relationship or anything else that you would like to be different.

❧ Write down all the things that bother you regarding this situation, all the things you would like to change.

❧ Then look at it, take a moment to think and write down positive thoughts that you would like to be able to think about it, emotions you would like to experience, and feelings that you would like to have in this situation.

❧ Every time you slip into thinking and wanting to act from the "old" way, choose to act from the "new" way and see what happens. You might experience change immediately; it might take a bit longer.

Notice how your emotions and feeling towards the situation you picked, change, how the situation changes (you might even want to write them down).

This is the exercise that helps to strengthen the belief that when we change the way we "see" things, the world around us changes. It helps to see in real life how things change, when we make changes within.

Have you noticed how some days we feel better than others and when we don't feel our greatest, more challenges happen in our life and days when we feel great, mostly good things happen to us? It happens because for one reason or another we have tuned into this kind of vibration. Everything counts –thoughts, our actions, our words and our choices of all kinds.

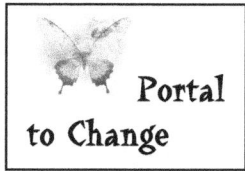

Becoming Aware Of The Vibration We Are In At This Moment And Time.

Portal to Change

What has been on my mind the most – today, yesterday, lately? Have I let distracting influences like the mainstream TV news and other people's opinions influence my own thoughts?

What choice of words do I mainly use? Positive? Negative?

Have I noticed a connection between the thoughts, feelings, emotions, words, situations I have been experiencing? What is the connection?

What have the emotions been behind my thoughts, words and actions?

THOUGHT   WORDS   ACTIONS   EMOTIONS

What are the most significant situations I have in my life at the moment?

What are the most significant people I have in my life at the moment and what makes them significant?

What kind of emotions and feelings do I have about certain situations in my life?

What kind of emotions and feelings do I have about relationships with different people in my life?

Look at the answers to the previous four questions and see if you can find the connection or pattern between your thoughts and feelings when it comes to certain situations and people in you life at the moment? What is it?

Am I happy with the way things are in my life? If not, what I would like to be different?

Do I believe others need to change in order for things to be different in my life?

Do I believe I need to change in order for me to have different experiences in life?

How can I change to experience the feeling I wish to experience? Can I change my thoughts, words and actions?

A great help in becoming more self-aware is to start journaling, writing down things that happen in your life and your feelings about them. Even if you feel like nothing "big" is happening write your thoughts and feelings about what that and perhaps what you would like to have happen. Doing this makes it possible to go "back in time", a valuable method to see a connection with the present situation and identify the patterns of our thinking that led to the current situation.

Allowing Time For Ourselves

When we meet new people and create new relationships with them, we invest our time and interest into the relationship and learn more about each other.

In order to become aware of our uniqueness and embrace it, we need to do the same with ourselves: We need to be a friend to ourselves. And we do it just like with any other relationship - we invest time and energy in getting to know ourselves.

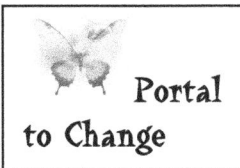

Portal to Change

Where to start and how? Let's start by taking an inventory of our life. We will identify and list our feelings and emotions, actions and reactions, choices we have made, beliefs we have, talents and gifts we have, accomplishments we are proud of, our priorities, things we have mastered, list as many as possible, it can be

149

an ongoing list.

To keep a list flowing consciously take a few deep breaths throughout the day. It sounds so simple and seemingly meaningless, but breathing is what keeps us alive in the first place and we usually take it for granted. Giving thanks and gratitude for being able to breathe and being alive is self affirming and leads to awareness.

Pay attention to how you breathe. Make a conscious attempt to balance your breathing – breathe out on the same count as breathe in (for example 10 seconds inhale and 10 seconds exhale). Then take a few minutes to become aware of how you feel. Scan your body and notice if there is any tension. Tension only means there has been some stuck energy and you can use conscious breathing to let go of tension. You do that by thinking of breathing into this part of your body.

Allow yourself to feel and ask: "How do I feel right now?" Notice how your body feels when you acknowledge your feelings during the day. How does it react to positive thoughts and feelings and to negative ones. Remember and know that no matter what kind of feelings come up – it's ok to have them. Just watch and listen for a while - you may even want to write down your experiences when you notice a difference.

Then ask yourself: "What area of my life needs the most attention at this moment and time?" and listen. The answer can come in many different ways – as a thought, as an idea, as a vision, memory, sound, smell or taste. The first thing you get is usually the answer or the key to the answer you are looking for. *(for more on this look in Chapter IX "Priorities")*

Being Honest With Ourselves

Do you feel like you are in the flow? Or do you feel tired of life and it seems like everything keeps you stuck, angry or frustrated?

Feeling stuck, tired, angry and frustrated are the primary clues that indicate we are not in alignment with our true selves. All of these feelings are lower vibrations. When we are not true to ourselves, we need more energy to invest into all we do as we are not in the flow, therefore it's natural to become tired more easily. When we are tired it's easier for us to feel stuck, angry and frustrated. Have you ever noticed how everything seems to go wrong during days and times when we don't feel our best? And how everything seems to be great when we are feeling good? It's just a shift in your energy.

When we are true to ourselves – we are in the flow, everything seems to flow easily and effortlessly. We don't need to invest energy into creating a dishonest life, so our energy is on a high level. When our energy is high, we are attracting other things in our life that are vibrating on a high level in all areas of life too.

We often believe that we can't afford to be true to ourselves for one reason or another. However that is just an illusion since our true essence is who we are meant to be which starts with being honest with ourselves on all levels if we want to succeed.

How to tell if we are truly honest or not? As mentioned before honesty is high vibrating energy therefore it is light, easy and flowing whereas a false image feels completely opposite and seems like life is suppressed. When we are honest with ourselves, we feel at peace with our choices, our life and all around us. When we are not honest we burden ourselves with sadness, depression, anxiety and in some cases a dead feeling inside. When we are honest – we know for sure but if we feel self-doubt and self-criticism, we need to pay attention to our instincts, our intuition and the signals from our body to best determine our truth and highest good.

Allowing Ourselves To Experiment

"What we mean by that is – be curious about life and what it has to offer, look around and notice even little things. It can be very easy to forget the beauty and uniqueness of all that there is in everyday life, but the same way – it can be very easy to remember the simple things of life and the beauty of it. It's all a matter of your choice"

People often have been afraid of changes, but that's the best part of life. Everything is changing – we are changing: the way we look, the way we dress, the way we think and speak, people we meet, beliefs we have, jobs we do, movies we watch… and in the same way, life around us is changing just on different level. What would happen if everything stayed the same?

It gives us the feeling of being stuck or going around in circles, but that's not what life is about.

Just to accept the fact that everything is changing is a step towards embracing changes. In times like we live now, there is not much space for holding onto the old. Have you noticed how from time to time some things in your life just don't work as they used to, even though you are handling them the same as always? Have you noticed how you don't seem to get along easily with people you used to get along with? Have you noticed how things that brought you joy in the past, don't bring you joy anymore? Think for example what you liked as a child and what you like now.

151

We can't escape changes even if we wanted to. My biggest question has been "Why are people afraid of trying new things and embracing changes, and is it possible to change that?"

If we look at life as if everything has a meaning, everything has it's purpose, and if we make an inventory of our life to see how different situations and relationships changed our life, it allows us to see more clearly how everything was great the way it was. If we can see the value of everything that happened in our life so far, we have moved beyond the ego mind and are more or less in the space of embracing new experiences. If we can't see how valuable everything in our life has been, we have been living in our ego. For some reason our mind has had the belief that changes are not good. What would happen if we would change this belief? The main reason has been the fear of taking responsibility.

As souls, we are free, but once we are born in a physical body, we have been given restrictions and rules in just about every area of life. We have been taught to follow rules and follow authorities. By conforming to other people's expectations and warp of life we can forget who we are our unique purpose in life. The more we become our own leader, the closer we come to being true. Every one of us is born a leader, the leader of our own lives, but the life long habit of following others might lead us to giving our personal power away.

By allowing our selves to change and open up to new possibilities – we are reclaiming our power as the leader of our own life and strengthening our uniqueness.

Portal to Change

Just for one day try this experiment. Commit to believe that changes are good and for better, and see what happens. You can simply say to yourself: *"Changes are good. I allow myself to believe that changes are good and bring blessings to everyone."* Every time you catch yourself thinking opposite – replace it with positive thoughts about changes. Notice how it makes you feel. Maybe you can do this on a day when you have less work to do as it is easier to focus and be present when we are in more "easy going" space.

Just for one day, as an experiment, choose to love yourself, choose to love others no matter what happens and choose to see the positive in everyone and everything. Say to yourself: *"Today I choose to love myself. I choose to see and recognize positive and good in me and in others. It is easy for me to love myself. The more I love myself the easier it is for me to love others. I love and I am loved."* See what happens when you do it.

See how it makes you feel. Choose to notice how it makes you feel, how you feel through out the day. You can put your hand over your heart when you say this to further bring love to yourself.

This is a process, one day at a time. Believe that we are always given enough information, enough tools to do what we are meant to do at every given moment, and as soon as we do step one, the sooner the instructions for step two are given.

We don't always need to know what follows; the important thing is that we trust the instructions we get as they are helping us to create the good life we desire.

CHAPTER IX

The Importance of Nurturing Ourselves

"If you want to be truly successful invest in yourself to get the knowledge you need to find your unique factor. When you find it and focus on it, and persevere your success will blossom."

- Sidney Madwed -

Nurture simply means to support. And we start with ourselves since it's not worth trying to help others if we haven't taken care of ourselves first.

We are who we are and can't be anything or anyone else. The same way – we can give only what we have, not what we don't have. Looking at it from physical perspective – if someone asks us for a cup of coffee, but we don't have one – we can't give it, if we are asked to give a book that we don't have, we can't give it simply because we don't have it.

The same idea works on a spiritual level: if someone asks me for healing, but I am not healed I can only give as much healing as I have healed myself. If I am asked to give peace – I can only give as much peace as I have, if I am asked to support someone or something – I can only support others if I am supporting myself, I can only give as much love as I have - not more than that. Of course we can help others even if we do have some stuff to work on (and we all do, all the time as it is part of life) but we can only help to the level that we have helped ourselves too.

This is also the way we attract different people in our lives, different situations and different emotions in our lives. The saying – like attracts like – really has proved to be true in many ways.

Have you ever noticed how two people can look at the same person or same situation and notice something completely different? If we wouldn't know it's the same thing, we would think they were talking about something different? And have you also noticed that there are times and situations where we see things similarly with others? Doesn't it usually happen to be so that we look at situations and the world around us more or less similar to our friends, people we are drawn to and more or less different to people who are not our friends?

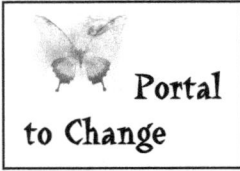

We Attract What We Focus On.

Portal to Change

Choose something: emotion, sound, feeling... and for one day tune in to it (with "tune in" I mean – do whatever helps you to visualize your chosen feeling, the most). Think about what you chose (I would suggest it's something positive), say it in your mind, feel it. Focus on it as much as you can and pay attention to your experiences during the day.

(for example: <u>emotion</u> – joy, happiness, positiveness, excitement; <u>sound</u> – car, doors opening and closing, birds singing, wind blowing, people talking; people using certain words as they speak...)

Notice how much more or less you notice anything related to your chosen "subject" and how much more or less you notice anything else around.

Do you see how much more you notice around you everything related to what you focus on rather than what you don't focus on?

It's just a simple way to experience the power of "law of attraction". You focus on something and you notice it more and on a deeper level.

Life's Web

Let's look at it from perspective of the Life's Web I wrote about earlier.

If we have experienced something – the thread has been created from us to everything related to our experience – emotion, feeling, people... When we come across something similar, we are familiar with it and therefore it's easier for us to relate. It also makes it easier for those who are on the other end of threads to come to us. Every thought we think, every action we take strengthens the thread.

The more similar threads we have with other people the more we relate to each other. If we and others choose to go a similar path for one reason

156

or another, we are in each other's life for longer time; if we move forward taking different directions, our connection gets weaker and weaker since we don't relate to each other so much anymore, and less and less similar threads are created in the future.

Having said all that – now back to nurturing ourselves from the Spider Web perspective. Everything happens for a reason and we always meet the people we are meant to meet, experience situations we are meant to experience. If the thread has been created from us to something or someone (when we look at it from the Spider Web perspective)– we are familiar with all related to this thread and it's easier for us to travel back and forth between each other (us and the situation that this thread leads). We can only relate to people that are on the similar level of nurturing themselves. We usually can help people who are in a lower space than we are as we have gone through similar experience ourselves and can relate. If we want to help someone who is in an energetically higher space of nurturing themselves, we aren't going to be able, because we have not created the way, yet, to this kind of nurturing experience for ourselves and therefore it's harder if not impossible to relate from the same perspective.

People always do their best to improve their life for the better. The more forward we move and better our life gets, the more it puts us into higher vibrating energy. When we are in alignment with who we are we are vibrating on a high level. Bottom line – if we want to live better, we do the best we can to move into higher vibrating energy realms. The higher we become energetically, more doors open in our lives because more threads/ connections are created therefore we can relate to more things and reach more people. The more we can relate and connect to, the more we can reach and help others and ourselves.

Knowing Ourselves

In order to embrace our uniqueness, nurturing ourselves is about knowing ourselves and our body: knowing what makes us feel good, makes us feel comfortable, knowing what's acceptable and not, knowing what is it that our body, spirit and mind need in order to feel good and allowing ourselves to receive it. Investing time and energy into receiving it. It's about honoring and respecting our needs and ourselves. To say it all in few words – nurturing ourselves is to love ourselves - to feel connectedness to all that is and feel the Universe within. It is like warm feeling inside our whole being where we know that all is well, we are safe and loved, it is when we do what makes us feel good in all aspects of life, when we don't try to prove or judge anything to anyone, that is where we just are.

Loving oneself is an art on its own. We don't always love from our hearts, we love, or think that we love, from our mind, but true love is possible only if we love from inside.

I have been very inspired by Louise L. Hay her "Mirror work" has been extremely helpful to me and many others when it comes to love ourselves. She suggests – you look in the mirror and say to yourself, to the person in the mirror – " I love you, (your name). I really, really love you!" what my experience shows, when you can do that and feel the words and feeling behind it resonate on all levels of your being – then you have come to the point where you truly love yourself.

"One very common thing that we see you doing is – believing that, when you try to please others, you show that you love them. That's not really the energy of love rather than feeding your ego. On the soul level, it is impossible to lie as our soul can see the truth no matter what. When you act from mind space instead of love, you can do nice things for others that make you feel good, but there is no feeling of love behind it and on soul level the other person can feel it too. There you can see that you have satisfied your ego, but it's not truly helping others. It's you caring for the "good feeling" instead of being love. This is also the case where you can feel not appreciated, where you feel like it wasn't worth it, where you feel sorry for yourself: "I am doing this for you, but this is what I get back! You don't care! ..." This is also a case of you trying to help by doing what you think is best for other person rather than allowing others to let you know what is the help they need.

Remember – there is more than one truth and what's right for you might be not right for person next to you. Imagine – you really, really want someone just to listen, no judgments, no advice, just listen but instead you are being told what to do or worst, what you have done wrong and what you should do... Do you feel good receiving what you didn't ask for? Do you feel like you have received help in your situation? Do you feel fulfilled and has it helped you to move forward?"

It is impossible to lie to ourselves and if we do not receive what we are looking for on the soul level, even with good intentions, the outcome is not so good at all. We might even feel frustrated and annoyed by what other person has been saying. Our mind might not be aware that it's not what I asked for, but our soul knows – all I wanted is someone to listen and hear me – no judgments, no advice. And so we walk away looking for what we need, somewhere else."

158

This leads to other important point in this topic – it's listening. When we do love ourselves – we listen to our body, we listen to our emotions and feeling, we listen to our intuition. Everyone of us knows about ourselves the best, we know what is it what we need in order to help us no matter what situation it is. If we love ourselves – we listen and hear the answers, we hear the guidance and then we can act. It's the same when it comes to loving others. If we love ourselves, we know how to listen, we also know how to not only listen, but also hear the best possible way to help other person. This way we do end up actually helping them rather than annoying them.

"When you love yourself, you accept yourself for who you are no matter what. You know that you are the best you that there is, you are doing the best you can in every situation and you know that so are the other people. Every one of you is doing their best. When you can see that, you can accept others and all they do on the highest level possible. Why do you wear the clothes you wear? Why do you say the words you say? Why do you act the way you do? Isn't it because you believe it to be the best way to be, act and handle the situation? Every one else is doing the same – they are living the best way possible from their understanding. Because everyone is different – everyone's best is different too."

We can expect for other person to act the way we would have acted, talk the way we would have talked, but this expectation is never met. When we can see and accept the fact that all of us are different and therefore all we do is different and unique from anyone else's doing, we have come to the space of unconditional love: loving ourselves and others.

When you are in a place where you accept and love yourself – the very natural process is to love your life as well, all aspects of it.

"We see it as fulfillment. It's like this – when you love yourself you are fulfilled, there is nothing more to be done in order to feel the love, it's there. The truth is – it's always there, but not all of you see or feel it but when you do, it gives the feeling of being fulfilled. It's like on the deepest being of your soul, your life has a meaning and you can feel it.

Now – you all seem to know that there has to be some meaning for your life otherwise – what's the point of living, but when you actually feel it, that's when all seems to start fall into place. (We will give you some tools to help you get there in a little moment.) Imagine you have a math problem to resolve – when you don't know how to resolve it nothing makes sense, you don't see the meaning of the numbers in problem but once you learn how to resolve it – you get to the answer and suddenly all makes sense. It's the same with the meaning of life – once you see and accept that everyone and everything has it's own purpose in life, and they take part in bigger picture, everything makes sense and gives fulfillment. Every step in the process of being is fulfilled and filled with love."

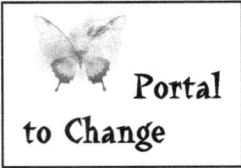

Portal to Change

Allow yourself few minutes time, close your eyes, take few deep breaths and say to yourself in your mind – "I love myself". Repeat it several times and notice how it makes you feel. Notice if there is any tension in your body. See if you can breathe in that part of your body and release the tension. Place your hand over your heart when you say this for extra self-nurturing.

Repeat this exercise as often as you feel like it.

This simple exercise is very helpful especially if you feel like you need to please someone even if it goes against your will, even if the action you would take wouldn't bring you positive feelings, when it's challenging for you to say "no". (If no other place, there is always a bathroom to go to where you can do it as it takes just a few minutes.) Doing this exercise puts you in the energy of love and allows you to be in touch with the true essence of you to make a decision based on who you are instead of who others would like you to be.

Loving ourselves also means loving unconditionally, without limits, judgments or expectations; loving ourselves just the way we are at this moment and time. There is nothing that needs to be changed in order for us to love ourselves. Of course there is always room for improvement, but here is the difference: We want to improve to be loved by others; or we want to improve because we love ourselves.

If we want to improve our lives – we choose to improve because we love. Love unconditionally where unconditional love means loving regardless of one's actions or beliefs.

When we love ourselves we know that we are love. Love comes from inside

When we truly love ourselves, we do it unconditionally. If we love it doesn't matter what size our body is, how big or small our nose is, or anything else, it doesn't matter what others or we ourselves think of us, how right or wrong we have done something, who are our friends, what our financial situation is… we love because we are love. If we remember that, there is nothing to prove to anybody.

Letting Go of The Old

Everything in life is changing all the time. There is nothing we can do to stop the changes that are happening around even if we try to avoid them and pretend that they are not happening.

Like the Spider Web, the more closely related, threads we have with someone or something, the more we are connected to them at a particular time. If for one reason or another we choose to be connected to different ideas and make threads to other people, we aren't connected so closely anymore and go separate ways. The connections we have made were necessary at the time, but if we don't resonate with them anymore, we block ourselves from making new connections and moving on.

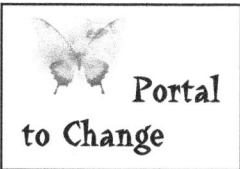

Portal to Change

Let's say you have a computer that works very well. Some time has passed and it is not working properly anymore or not working at all. Wouldn't you rather let go of it and get a new one? You need to make space for a new one to come. If the old computer is still there, where would you put the new one? If you keep it right where it is, you need to find a place for new one, but if you keep hold onto old things like this computer, for instance, soon your place would be filled with stuff that doesn't have any practical use and only brings confusion. The same applies to emotions, feelings, beliefs, friends… anything in our lives.

With every day that passes, we have more and more experiences on different levels of life. We can't really undo on a physical level what we have experienced, what we have said, how we have felt as it's part of who we are, but we can let go of attachments on an energy level. With

161

"attachments on energy level" I mean – holding onto situations, emotions, feelings, relationships that don't serve us anymore.

How to know if they serve us or not? Life is about having fun and enjoying all we do. If something makes us feel good it helps us to enjoy what we do, enjoy life. If we feel good and uplifted, positively charged by the situation we are in, by people we are hanging out with, by emotions we are feeling and by anything that's going on in our life, it serves us (works both ways, we serve them too as there is always a balance). If we feel drained, angry, frustrated, pessimistic, tired when we are in some particular situation or hanging out with certain people, focusing on certain emotions, feelings, experiences – that's a clear indicator that something is not working for us anymore. Usually we already know what is it we need to let go, we know what brings out the positive in us, what the negative – it's only a matter of us taking action and actually letting go. For those people who feel exhausted, tired and pessimistic and don't know what causes it, the great thing to do would be to make and inventory of their life and examine believes influences and past events to discover those moments that have had a negative impact on them in order to achieve what they would rather have instead.

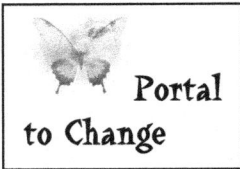

Portal to Change

What's Working in My Life and What's not Anymore

Make a list for bringing your attention to what's working well in your life (yourself, family, situations, people, job, believes and others) and what's not working anymore ("working" here means – you feel great about the way things are, "not working" means, you used to feel great about the way things were, but not anymore):

162

(While working on checklist, remember to imagine that there is a Fairy Godmother with her Magic wand in front of you who is taking care of all "but's" and "what if's").

🦋 Do I love myself just the way I am, do I love myself unconditionally?
- Congratulations to you, if you can truly say and feel "yes"!
-Congratulations to you, if you can't say "yes" as there are many "checkpoints" to come that help to bring clarity and become aware of steps to take towards loving yourself!
🦋   What is it about myself that I like?

✿   What is it about myself that I don't like?

✿   Invest a few minutes by going through everything that you wrote here: Take a deep breath and say in your mind (you can say it out loud as well if you prefer):
"I accept that I don't like... (take one thing from your list)... about myself and I am willing to let it go now."
Go through every single thing in your list one by one. Accepting what you don't like shows that you acknowledge it, honor it, but are willing to let it go in peace.

✿   What is it I do not like about my life?

- Invest a few minutes by going through everything that you wrote here: take a deep breath and say in your mind (you can say it out loud as well if you prefer): *"I accept that I don't like... (take one thing from your list)... about my life and I am willing to let it go now."* Go through every single thing in your list one by one.

164

What is it that I like about my life the way it is now?

When do I feel the happiest?

When do I feel my worst?

- Invest a few minutes by going through everything that you wrote here: take a deep breath and say in your mind (you can say it out loud as well if you prefer): **"I accept that I feel the worst, when...** *(take one thing from your list)...* **and I am willing to let go of what causes me feel this way, now."** Go through every single thing in your list one by one.

🦋 Who are the people in my life who I enjoy the most?

🦋 Who are the people in my life who I enjoy the least?

Invest a few minutes by going through everything that you wrote here: take a deep breath and say in your mind (you can say it out loud as well if you prefer): **"I accept that I feel this way about you and I am willing to let go of that part of me which** (any particular feeling you have about this person, "gets angry" for instance) **when I think of you/talk to you/hang out with you (here you can say any situation/reason that causes you to feel about this person the way you feel).** Go through every single thing in your list one by one.

🦋 Do I love my job?

🦋 If your answer was "no" to this question, remember Fairy Godmother who is taking care of all "but's and what if's" and imagine job you would love to do?

🦋 If you have challenges imagining your ideal job, make a list of all the things you are good at and enjoy doing! Look at your list and see if any job comes to your mind now!

I AM GOOD AT:

🦋 Do I enjoy my family?

🦋 What about my family do I enjoy?

🦋 What do I not enjoy about my family?

- Explore the idea that family members have the greatest lessons to learn and teach as they are the closest people in our life. Looking at the answers to the previous questions, take time to see if you can make a connection between what you don't like about your family/any family member and you/your personal life/feelings/emotions/experiences...

🦋   Is there balance in my life between work and free time/ family and friends?

🦋   If the answer to the previous question was "no", say in your mind or out loud:
"I accept that my life has been out of balance and I am willing to allow balance in my life now."
Take time to think if there is anything you could do differently, something you might not have tried before, something you might find interesting.

🦋   Now that you have gone through these questions and invested some time and energy into focusing on them, what are your thoughts and ideas about:
-what is working for you (in any area of life)?

-what is not working in your life anymore (any area)?

(here you can say: "I accept that this is not working in my life anymore – read all that's on your list – and I am willing to let go of it now. I am willing to embrace new opportunities in my life, I am willing to move forward with ease right now.")

Important to remember: When you think of what you would like to have in your life, now that you have let go of the old, focus on feelings – think: *"How is it I want to feel, how do I envision myself feeling when I have in my life what I want?"*

Investing Time In Our Priorities

In order to embrace our uniqueness, it's important to look at all aspects of ourselves, which includes knowing what our priorities are and accepting them.

When looking at priorities, the most important thing is to become clear if our priorities are truly ours or if we have chosen them to be priorities based on outside influences. What I mean by that is with so many possibilities and opportunities in today's world, it might be easy to rely on TV, media, our parents believes, society's customs, co-workers, teachers, neighbors … and peer groups. However, it's only when we are true to ourselves and choose priorities based on our beliefs and our whole being, that we are taking care of ourselves and nurturing our soul and spirit.

	Priorities
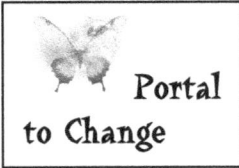 Portal to Change	Following is an exercise that helps bring clarity on what our priorities are.

Before you start, please be willing to allow yourself to listen to your true self and hear it (this might take some practice). You can do it by saying: *"I am willing to allow myself to listen to my true self and my true feelings. I am willing to hear myself"* (and remember deep breathing).

Then:

Make a list of your priorities, the ones that you are having as priorities in your life at present time (the ones you put the most attention to)!

Then look at them one by one (keep in mind – the Fairy Godmother with her magic wand is taking care of all the concerns and worries, buts and what ifs)
-Does this priority make your heart sing?

-Is this priority really yours, is it something you inherited from others (family, relatives, friends, boss, work…) or an expectation from you?

🦋 Now write down at least 4 absolute priorities. Imagine that anything is possible – what would your priorities be?

🦋 Take time to look at them one by one again and look how much time you invest into your priorities.

Keeping your mind wide open think if there is any way you could allow yourself more time and effort for your priorities.

Taking Care of Our Body

We are the soul in a human body; it's our vehicle during this lifetime. What we put in it, how we treat it, will affect how this vehicle will look and work.

Think of a car – even an old car could look like new if appropriate care has been given it and a new car can look old if not cared for well. It's up to us what kind of tools we use to keep our car in great shape just as it's up to us, what kind of tools we use to take care of our body.

We have talked about taking care of ourselves spiritually. This is about taking care physically and starting from within, starting with what we put into our bodies, how we nurture our bodies with food and exercises.

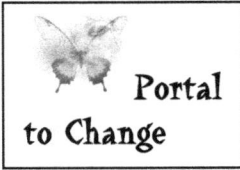

	Some Focal Points To Bring Awareness To:
Portal to Change	What are my eating habits?

What kind of food do I eat?

What am I drinking throughout the day?

🦋 Do I give consideration to what I eat, and how I eat?

🦋 Do I plan for and prepare the food myself or do I let others do it for me? What do I prefer?

🦋 Do I eat because I feel I have to or because I want to?

🦋 Do I eat when I feel like eating or do I eat whenever I have time?

🦋 Do I eat when I am really hungry or do I use eating as a delay tactic to avoid doing something meaningful?

🦋 Do I follow a diet?

🦋 If I am dieting – what is the main reason I chose this particular diet?

❧   Do I listen to how body reacts when I eat and when?

❧   Are my eating habits truly mine (meaning they represent my true essence) or have I adopted them from someone or somewhere else? Write down your thoughts on this!

❧   If I could choose to change anything in my eating habits, what would it be?

❧   If I would listen to my body's messages – what food would my body benefit from and what beverages?

It doesn't matter what is it we are eating or when we are eating, what matters is that we listen to our body's needs.

We have unique bodies as well as unique needs when it comes to food. This is why it is important to pay attention to our body.

Our body's natural state is to be healthy and the body itself is natural. From an energy standpoint, the more natural the food, the higher vibrating energy it has. The more we vibrate on a higher frequency and are surrounded by higher energy the better we can see into any aspect of our life. It's like with water: its natural state is to be clear but the more less natural things we add to it, the murkier it gets.

Even if you have never had experience with babies, you might have seen that babies are fed lots of fruits and vegetables that is more natural than adults eat. Why is that? – Their bodies are vibrating high since they have not been exposed yet to unnatural products and therefore can process only high vibrating foods. Then kids are introduced to other kinds of food with lower frequencies like red meat and sugar. It's no surprise that babies are advised to avoid these foods (as mentioned before – the more processed foods are the lower vibrating they are). But as children get older it's said to be safe to introduce them to other foods. Everyone of us has been a child and we might know from our own experience – the older we grew, the more we were exposed to a greater variety of everything that's around and available.

As grownups/ parents/ guardians if we honor children for being their unique selves and we honor their inner wisdom, we might be amazingly surprised by their choice in food. Children seem to know exactly what they want and when they want to eat. As strange as it may sound – their first choice is usually a healthy one, not candy and junk foods as we may think it would be.

As children grow up they adapt to the environment they are in and their eating habits conform to the people around them.

As more children are introduced to lower vibrating foods their energy becomes lower with all that's related to it including challenges in one or more aspects of life.

What if we crave lower vibrating foods and we love them? It's great if that's what our body really wants and needs, and we don't eat these foods because we feel like we have to. We don't usually crave the same foods all the time, which is a clear example that body needs different foods to support us (as well as other way around). If we notice what foods are we craving from time to time and compare them to what we are going through in our life at that time – we might find a pattern.

It can be easy to follow external influences like other family members, friends, ads on TV, radio or online, and their ideas about what's best for us. However following these sources doesn't support the process of embracing our uniqueness and getting in touch with who we are.

Instead, we can adjust outside ideas to fit in with what we know in our heart to be true rather than compromising our truth and beliefs to fit outside ideas.

Once we know how to listen to our body, the next step is to stick with it which might be even more challenging, but since anything is possible, so is the idea of sticking with what you know to be true and working for your body. If this is all new to you, it's important to remember that in most cases changes don't happen overnight and with no effort.

Another part of taking care of your body is physical activities. Have you ever noticed how much children move around and how they seem to never get tired? And have you ever noticed how natural being active is for children? And how less active many of us become as older we get?

Being physically active is our natural state as well as state of being in high vibrating energy. To do physical activities is as necessary as eating and drinking since it helps our body to be in a flow, it keeps energy moving and touches every cell in our body that way keeping it alive.

We have a lot of energy centers (also known as chakras) in our body – some of them bigger some smaller. There are 7 main energy centers and each one of them is related to different emotions, different body parts. The energy center that is under our ribcage represents our inner power – it's called Solar Plexus, inner wisdom, and our true essence.

How often do we pay attention to how we breathe? The fact is – if our breath is shallow, we breathe in our chest; if we take a deep breath – we breathe with our belly. Every time we breathe in – we let the fresh, new energy enter our body, every time we breathe out – we let the old, used energy out. Since our true essence, soul, is energy, it's natural for our true self to be recharged through breathing.

When we do physical exercises whatever they might be, our breath naturally tends to become deeper and we tend to breathe through the belly – our inner power center. Since our inner power center is the most important, it's where our true self lives from, it's important for this part of body to have plenty of fresh energy. It's important for this part of the body to be regularly recharged especially if we have chosen to be true to ourselves. The more freshness it receives, as more clarity it brings to our whole being – mind, body and spirit.

Practice Belly Breathing

Portal to Change

The best way to see if we are breathing deeply into our belly is, to stand in front of mirror and watch ourselves. When we inhale ideally the belly expands like a balloon. It's important to notice the shoulders since they tend to go up as we inhale, however, for a "belly breath" important is for the shoulders to stay down and that's where mirror is a great help!

To feel if your belly gets like a balloon when you breathe in put your hand on your belly when you breathe.

When you exhale, pull the belly in, feel the balloon shrinking.

What kind of physical activities we do is not as important as that we do something physically active. Usually we already know what we prefer. If we are not sure yet, there are always opportunities to find out what works the best. And here is a hint: It's usually the activity that goes by so fast that we don't notice the time.

CHAPTER X

Honoring the Power Within

"We travel the world and look around in search of what we believe we need, and find it within."

- Author Unknown -

Inner Power

Inner power is our knowingness and ability to act coming from inside of us.

Being told what to do and what not from the moment we are born makes it so much easier to adopt the belief that our power lies outside of us, but how can it?

When we think, we talk, we act, we sing we sleep, or do anything we do it ourselves. We have the awareness of the ability to do these things as well as some kind of power to do them. Just the fact that thought can be formed in our mind, words can be picked to form the thought, words can be said and chosen to show that we have some kind of power that is within. To move our physical body, we have to have some power too or we would not be able to move.

The more we practice, the stronger we get. As children we learn to talk by practicing talking and listening it. When we learn to walk, the more we practice, the better we get. We go to the gym, the more we practice the stronger we get.

No matter what it is we do, we have to have some kind of willingness to do that. We might allow ourselves to be influenced by outside sources when making the choice to do what we are doing but even then we must have some kind of power to allow ourselves to be influenced. It's not like we have a physical cord coming out of us and we plug ourselves into socket to get power from there. It's the power that lies within.

A power that helps us to not only see, hear, smell or act but also intelligence that helps us to process what we have experienced, put it together and make choices based on our experience, a power that allows us to trust our intuition, a power that allows us to move forward in life and take action.

Each one of us has this power within and more or less we are using it all the time. It's our own responsibility how we are using it and how we are going to use it.

Our ability to make decisions, take action and handle any task is our inner strength. It's our ability to overcome fear, negative temptations and habits, destructive patterns, willingness to change and move forward in life, ability to stand our ground, follow the guidance we receive.

It also goes hand in hand with self discipline/ self control which is inner strength that helps us to stick to our decisions, actions and plans no matter what happens – it's when we say *"I am willing to do whatever it takes"* and we stick with it all the way through. It is what helps us to overcome difficulties and helps us to achieve our goals, make our dreams come true.

Portal to Change

Increase Your Inner Power

Here are a few ideas on what to pay attention to when working to increase and develop inner power (you may want to write down what you get when you read, think and focus on following ideas as it is the way you invite them more into your life):

focus on what you are good at.

do things that make you feel fulfilled.

refuse to satisfy unhealthy desires

do things that you have felt like doing already for a while but haven't done yet

act as if you already have overcome any challenges in your life, as if you are already where you want to be, you have what you would like to have

allow yourself to accept the possibility to change

say "no" for a change

accept somebody in your life and their actions for who they are without judging or "labeling"

find and see something positive in your worst "enemy"

find something positive to say in seemingly bad situation, to someone you don't get along with

- take few deep breaths throughout the day
- take few moments to accept the way you feel at this very moment
- take a few moments to notice how you really feel about any particular situation or person and allow yourself to accept your feelings
- make a phone call you have wanted to make for a long time
- find and feel the joy in what you do

The more practice you get, the stronger your inner power becomes. Practice every day by taking one step at the time doing simple things like:
- skip watching TV and go for a walk
- use stairs instead of elevator
- drink water instead of Soda
- eat vegetables instead of sweets
- take dog for a walk instead of asking someone else to do it
- some day wake up earlier than you are used to

Breathing

Conscious breathing can be the most simplest and challenging thing.

Once we are consciously aware of our breathing, we are present. But this is where breathing might become challenge because we don't always pay attention to our breathing, we forget.

Breath is what keeps our entire planet alive and breathing is so natural that often we take it for granted.

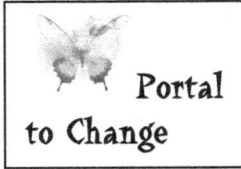

Breathe

Pay attention to your breathing throughout the day. Notice how your breathing is, if you breathe in and out the same amount of air or is your inhalation longer than your exhalation, (or other way around).

Breathing in and out represents giving and receiving. Ideally they are balanced and what we can do is, focus on breathing in on the same count and breathe out on the same count (for example 10 seconds to inhale and 10 seconds to exhale).

When you breathe consciously notice how air comes into your body, how your body expands, how incoming air touches cells in your body. When you breathe out, consciously notice how your body contracts and lets go of air that's not needed anymore.

Being Present

Being present means being aware of all that is happening now. If you are reading these lines and are fully focused on what you read, you are present. As soon as our mind starts to wonder around, you lose touch with now.

We invest a lot of time into living in the past (re-thinking, re-talking about what happened, what should have been said, done, what shouldn't have…) and future (what is happening later, what's for dinner, what am I going to say, do…). Of course, to a degree it is needed, but if we always focus on past or future, then what happens to the present?

Life's Web

When we are in the middle, we are present with our whole being and therefore our power. As soon as thoughts about the past or future come up, the thread is being created and "present" energy is being given away to past or future. The more we focus on past and future, the more threads are created and less energy is left for '"being present" and in our power.

Being present is what many people refer to as quality time.

Have you heard the idea that it's not about how much time you invest doing something, it's about the quality of time that you invest?

Being with children in the best way to connect with "living in the now". Children are the greatest teachers of how it is done. All that there is for them is now. Have you ever been in a situation or witnessed the situation where grownups are with kids in the same room, seemingly spending time with kids talking, but their mind wanders somewhere else? Or they say they spend time with their kids, but they do it grownup's way: they do what seems important and fun to them instead of asking their kids what's important to them.

Even if we invest a short amount of time in being present with children, doing what's meaningful to them, on energy level it creates a space for children to be present and more receptive to do things we ask them to do, for example: clean up their toys, get ready for bed...

The same is with living in the present moment. To a degree it's important to be aware of the connection with past and future. When we invest only a small amount of time being present, it's much easier to incorporate this "being present" into life that is combination of past, present and future.

Life's Web

When we are just born, living in the present moment is all we know – that's us in the middle. The older we get, the easier it might be to lose touch with "being present" as there is more past and more threads and connections made, more for a mind to wander around in. There is always a past and the future with it's possibilities as we are the part of us, but if we can see past and future and stay present - we stay in the middle, our power, our center. We don't give our power away to the past or future... only 'now".

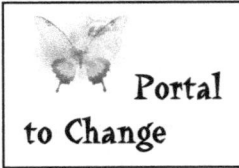

✿✿ Portal to Change	"Being Present" Exercise ✿ Sit comfortably ✿ Close your eyes and take few deep breaths.

✿ Focus on your body starting with the crown of your head

✿ Then slowly move your attention down your body:

✿ Back of head, your face, eyes, nose, ears, chin, neck, shoulders…

✿ Arms, elbows, hands and feel every finger.

✿ Move your attention to your chest, heart, your belly, your back.

✿ Move attention down to your hips, thighs, knees, shins, feet…

✿ Feel every toe and anything that your feet are touching.

✿ Now feel your body as whole – all at once. If there is any part you have a challenging time feeling, breathe in it – when you breathe, imagine you are breathing through that part of your body.

✿ Notice things around you, where you are, what you are standing or sitting on, sounds you can hear, notice what you can smell.

✿ Breathe it all in and notice how it makes you feel.

The more you practice this exercise, the easier it becomes to feel your body and everything around you within a few moments, this helps you to be present with your body which is a key to being present in all aspects of life.

✿ ⚘ ❀ ⚘ ✿

Trusting Our Intuition

All of us have intuition. It is our ability to sense and know without any visible reason, it's our ability to receive guidance and messages without any visible source. It's that feeling and guidance we get to do something, say something, go somewhere, that doesn't really make any sense, however it's strong and persistent. If we don't follow it, we later learn that if we had followed it would have helped us in one way or another. If we follow this feeling and take action, we learn the benefits and see how it makes sense later.

Very simple example – before going out of the house, you feel guided to take an umbrella. The weather forecast says that it's going to be sunny all day, the sky is clear blue and it really doesn't make sense to take an umbrella... A few hours later, it rains. If you followed your intuition and took an umbrella with you, good for you, if you followed your mind, which told you that it doesn't make sense to bring an umbrella good for you, too. Either way the Universe is showing us and confirming that even though the idea didn't make sense at the beginning, the information that we got was valuable. The more we become aware of these messages and see how they make sense later, the more opportunity we have to learn to trust our intuition.

Our intuition is also the one that gives us quick insight into any situation, any relationship, any area of life to help us and anyone else involved. It's that feeling we get when someone is not telling the truth, when we feel that something is not right even though we don't see yet, what exactly it is, when we feel our loved one is in trouble (especially parents about their children).

Often we receive this knowledge unconsciously. Because this ability to know and awareness of it is a part of who we are it happens naturally without any conscious effort. Knowing ourselves enough and being aware of this knowledge that we have, is what helps us to experience intuitive guidance more and more. Tap into it. It helps us to be aware of how to consciously access this knowing.

Making The "Right" Choices

Everything in our life is choice. There are unlimited possibilities around us in this world.

In any situation that we are, in any aspect of life, there is a variety of options available – one more preferable than the others. We have the power to choose.

All our choices are created within us: thoughts we choose to think, words we choose to speak, and actions we choose to take... We might feel influenced by others in many aspects of life, might be afraid to let others know our true selves, might feel threatened to make the choice that represents our true self, but no matter what, there is no such thing as "right" or "wrong" choices.

We might have thought or been taught that there is a right and wrong, but only our ego respond to this kind of teaching. Often we tend to believe that our truth and beliefs are the only absolute truth, but the fact is – since we are all different and unique, there is no possible way that the choice that is "right" for one person would be "right" for another (same goes for wrong choices).

Everyone of us knows what is the "right" choice for us in any given situation since this knowing resides within. For instance someone introduces us to a new diet. We might choose to try it, but if we don't like it, we won't choose it ever again. Not because of the outside source, but because of the experience we have had. Our choice is based on our experiences, memories and feelings. One choice might feel better than other, but even the choice that seems to bring the greatest challenges is the "right" choice as it is teaching us a lesson.

Everyone of us is doing our best in any given situation. Our "best" changes with every moment depending on other aspects of our lives. For instance, if we had a little sleep, we might be not able to concentrate/focus as well as if we had a good sleep. However, even with little sleep we are doing our best to focus. Our "best" in this case is not the same "best" as when we have had a good nights sleep.

The more we accept our uniqueness, the more we are able to see uniqueness in others, which also helps to see how unique our choices are.

The **right choice** is one that is the most appropriate for person making it.

Right Choice

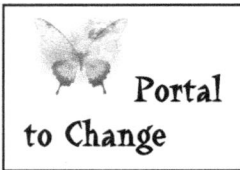
Portal
to Change

How to know if the choice we are making is the right one?

🦋 The best thing is to focus on the situation that requires a choice

🦋 Imagine that there is a Fairy Godmother in front of you and she is taking care of all "but's" and "what if's" – allow her to take care of them in your situation.

🦋 Now that that's taken care of, focus on the situation again and feel it. What is the feeling that comes up? What is the feeling you would like to have?

🦋 What can you do to feel the way you would like to feel?

186

❦ What do you feel like doing in this situation now that all "but's" and "what if's" are taken care of?

❦ From all the possible choices, which one is the one that makes you feel good and feels right?

Once we know in our heart what our "right" choice is, the next step is to take an action.

❦ ❦ ❦

When we think of life in general – what is it that makes our heart sing? What is it that makes your heart sing? How do we want to feel? How do you want to feel?

It's not what we say in our life, what matters, it's how we feel. Words might not always show the truth however our choice of action does. If we say we don't like watching TV but we keep watching it, our action shows that we do like to watch TV. Why would otherwise we choose to watch? If we say we don't like to drink coffee, but we keep drinking it, our action shows that we still like it.

It's only when our actions match with our words, we are in alignment with who we are. When we are present, it's easier for us to know what to do and what is it we want to do.

Always listen to your heart when making a choice and remember that it's impossible to make anything else than "right" choice for you. When it comes to other people – it's only up to them to decide, what's the "right" thing to do.

Standing Our Ground

Once we are aware of our inner power, our inner strengths, knowing ourselves and are aware of our choices, the next step is to stick with what we know to be true and don't settle for less.

When we are honest with ourselves, we know what our true desires are. However there is always a chance that other people might try to talk us out of it and betray our true feelings and desires.

Your feelings, thoughts, dreams and desires are valuable and there is no reason for letting influences from outside to let you go away from them. It's important to speak our truth and let others know how we feel. When we do that, new solutions appear, and it's easier to find the situation that works out for everyone involved.

If we don't allow ourselves to say how we feel, to express ourselves, if we don't pay attention to our true feelings, they get stored within us one by one and block the energy flow. The more blocked energy there is, the more challenges we experience in our life, the less happy we are. However, when we let others know our true feelings and allow ourselves to express who we are, it's us showing respect to ourselves and increasing our self-confidence. We can only receive respect from others if we respect ourselves.

Spirit Realm says: "Standing your ground is the most powerful thing that you can do for yourself. It puts everything into a new perspective; it allows freedom in your life and in the life of others. It's not that your truth is better than other people's truth, it's about loving yourself enough to accept your truth, allowing your truth and true self to be heard as well as allowing others to speak their truth.

It's also about acceptance, when you fully accept who you are, only then you are able to let go of fear to speak your truth."

CHAPTER XI

Going Beyond Limitations and Enjoying Freedom

"What each must seek in his life never was on land or sea. It is something out of his own unique potentiality for experience, something that never has been and never could have been experienced by anyone else."
- Joseph Campbell -

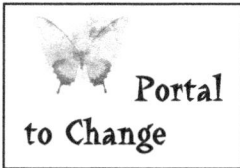

Being Free

Portal to Change

I am free!

Get comfortable and take few deep breaths. Allow yourself to relax and focus on freedom: just in your mind say "freedom" for few times, also "I am free", "It's my Divine right to be free!"

☙ Notice how it makes you feel.

☙ In your mind say to yourself several times: *"I am open to unlimited possibilities!"*

☙ Notice again how it makes you feel.

☙ Another affirmation to say: *"I am willing to go beyond limitations and enjoy freedom in my life!"*

☙ Notice how this makes you feel.

☙ Experiment with different positive affirmations (make up your own) related to "freedom", allow yourself to feel the freedom and be in this freedom energy for as long as it feels "right".

☙ Then, open your eyes.

Freedom is our Divine right and the meaning of it is – living without limitations.

There seems to be a lot of thought given to limiting ourselves and when we look at it, it can be very understandable. When we are born into this planet, our physical body gives our soul a form. Whenever something has been given a form, there is a limitation.

We experience limitation when our mind (ego) tells us that we can't have, can't do something or that something is impossible. And it's not only our mind, it might be people around us, we might see it on TV, hear it on Radio, read in a newspaper. On the Soul level, there are no limits to what is possible and what is not, but having an experience as a human we often forget as our ego tends to be louder and overpower our soul.

Whenever we have the urge to experience something new, learn something new on one level or another, we have recognized the limitation and are willing to overcome it.

Life's Web

If we look at it from "spider web" idea:
Being born in this human body puts us in the middle of the spider web. The more we live as humans, the more limitations we experience. The younger we are, the more we are in touch with freedom that is our Divine right: we want to and we go beyond limitations and as a result, as children we often hear: "don't go there, don't do that, don't touch it, you can do it when you grow up, it's not for small children, stop it" as well as "do this, do that, go there, come here, bring this, this is how it's done, this is what you do, this is how you do it" and many others.

We experience more limitations as we grow up: in kindergarten, school, work, society, in any place we go. Other people tell us how to behave, what to do, how to do, telling us what's right and what's wrong (often from their point of view but believing that it's the only right thing to do for everyone), we are being told what to say, how and when.

As we experience more limitations, more threads in our life web are being created leading to limited experiences. If we focus on limitations, we create an easier way for limiting energy to flow between us. The more we stay in our power, the more we are connected with who we are, with our truth even though we experience limitations and their resulting, they don't overtake our life because we are aware of unlimited possibilities and of our Divine right to freedom. In other words, the ego based beliefs about limitations are there in our web, but they don't have power over us.

Of course, we don't mean here that limitations are not needed, in healthy doses they are very great, like a speed limit for example, rules for driving, rules in school, work, rules that are putting some limits... they are needed everywhere. There has to be some order and therefore there are limitations that are healthy.

It's only when we allow them to create the belief within us that everything has limits and there is no complete freedom possible, only then the idea about limitation can be destructive and that's what we are trying to bring to awareness.

For instance: Because there are some rules that put limitations on but are important to follow, we might develop the belief that not everything is possible and apply this belief when we think of ourselves, being true to ourselves, speaking our truth, standing our ground, being who we are, sticking to what we believe is right and more. This is what we mean by 'going beyond limitations": getting in touch with our true self, our soul, remembering that anything is possible that we are free to make any choice we want and live the life of our dreams. We are free to accept who we are and be accepted for who we are, we are free to be our gorgeous and unique selves not only on a soul level but also on the physical level.

Embracing our uniqueness is making friends with who we are. It's awareness of who we are, it's loving any aspect of ourselves and our life, respecting ourselves, it is honoring the light within us and every living being. When we are happy, everyone around us feels happier too.

It's accepting that we have a physical body, looking beyond the limitations that it might create and being aware of endless possibilities, being aware of the freedom to live our life to the fullest.

Feeling Safe

"I trust the process of the Universe and I am safe!" I believe is the most powerful mantra for feeling safe.

On the soul level all of us know that we are always taken care of no matter what situation we would be in. On another hand our mind has a different idea.

Life's Web

Being in the middle of the Life Web, we are who we are and we know that we are safe. Every time we experience limitations on the soul level, we still know that it is safe to be who we are, but the thread is created to this limitation and door open to it. The more we focus on limitations that we come in contact with in our life, the stronger the thread becomes which causes us to have stronger belief in limits and limitations. That's one of the strongest reasons for our belief in limitations being born in this lifetime.

Ideally we would avoid feeding limiting energy with our beliefs rather just leaving it alone.

Imagine that the middle of your life's Web is higher than sides. You are part of all that there is and not affected by lower energies even if threads have been created.

Letting Go Of Masks

Have you ever experienced that you act differently in certain situations or with certain people? For instance, finding our that your parents will come over for dinner, you clean the house, make everything look better than ever, tell your partner/ children what to say or what to not say, hide certain books you have that might cause challenging conversations, feel angry but show a happy face anyway. These are just few examples of masks that we often wear throughout our life.

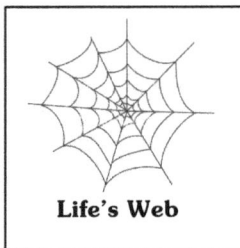
Life's Web

In the middle, we are who we are without any masks. In order to pretend to be someone or something we are not, there needs to be a belief that it's not safe to be who we are whether it would be in certain situations or with certain people. The more we pretend to be who we aren't, more threads are created that lead to this specific situation and anything related to it. The more threads there are leading to different masks that we show to the world, the more energy and power is taken

192

away from who we truly are - there is less left for expressing our true selves.

In true essence we are still who we are – our unique selves, we have just put on a mask believing that it's better and safer to wear it instead of showing our true self. Often we might even have a collection of masks for each situation and person in our life.

The more masks we wear the easier it is to get tangled in all the threads of pretense and forget who we truly are. It's like an illusion: we believe this is who we are, this is the only way of living.

Not everyone is aware of wearing masks as it depends on many factors. If we feel like we can't be who we are for one reason or another, we have given our power of freedom away; we have given our power to be who we are away. We have limited ourselves or we've allowed ourselves to believe that we have to limit ourselves.

In order to embrace our uniqueness it's important to let go of all the masks that we have created.

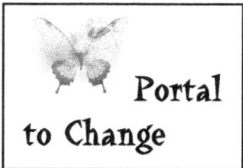

Masks

> **Portal to Change**

Is there any time, any situation where you feel like you are true to yourself, not pretending to be someone else (either it's with just being by yourself or in connection with someone or something)?

If yes, write down what it is.

✿ Now focus on different aspects of your life and think. Allow yourself to see, <u>where you are not being true, where you could say, you are wearing masks</u>. In what kind of situations, with what kind of people… maybe there are certain topics that invoke the feeling of the need for putting a mask on.

✿ Look at what you have written and see if you find similarities – do you wear masks with similar people, the similar situations or are they completely different?

Now go through the list of places and situations where you don't wear masks: what do you believe allows you to be free of masks in these situations? Write them down.

Go through the list of situations and places you wear masks: what do you believe is a reason for you to wear masks in these situations?

Remember about the Fairy God mother who is right by your side taking care of all the "but's" and "what if's"! What would be your ideal action in situations where you have been "wearing" masks? What steps can you take in order to let go of masks?

One step at a time!

Taking Charge of Our Life

Taking charge of our life simply means: To live consciously. It is all about taking full responsibility for every thought we think, every word we say, every action we take, every choice we make.

With all that is said above and in previous chapters: when it comes to embracing our uniqueness the most important thing for all of us to remember is that we are fully 100% responsible for our life and it's not only about remembering, it's about claiming this responsibility and taking action.

Many of you may have heard about Dr. Masaru Emoto and his experiment with water where he scientifically proved that every word, even if it's only a thought in mind or written, affects water. He proved that positive words, positive emotions turn water into beautiful snowflake like crystals but negative words and thoughts turn water into disfigured forms.

Thoughts, words, emotions, ideas are seeds of action – they are all within us, they are born within us. The human body is 75% water – just one tiny word affects the water and therefore 75% of us. One word affects us, one thought, one emotion, one idea… the combination of all our thoughts, words, deeds creates a unique blend of crystals that are within us and we live from this unique space in this world.

The thoughts are born within us, the words we speak come out of our mouth, the emotions we feel are within us, we can only take action if for one reason or another we choose to do so. Also on the soul level – we chose to come to this planet. It all comes from within.

Since it all comes from within and since we are the owners of our inner power – we are also the only ones who are responsible for how we use this power. We are responsible for our choices: Choice of thoughts, words, feelings, and actions. In other words we are in charge of ourselves and what happens in our life. Even if we have chosen to believe that someone else is in charge of our life, we are responsible for making that choice, too.

Life's Web

We are souls who chose to come to Earth to have a human life. Once we are born we experience being told from others around us what to do. We are in the middle of the "Life's Web" when we are just born. The more we are told what to do and the more people we meet in our lives, the more situations we are in. The more threads to the web are created.

Growing up everything that someone else says (parents, teachers, people around, relatives, friends, society...) make the threads stronger. The threads create the space for us to give our power of "being in charge of our life" away. But it doesn't have to be this way!

Listening to adults and teachers or our employers does not always mean we give our power away. Just like with having rules, as long as it is reasonable and is for highest good to all involved, it is actually needed.

However when our only experience is to blindly follow directions and those are the only threads that have been created in our "life web", our true self becomes increasingly suppressed and hidden. This is where we often start to live outside our body. Of course, in a way we are in our body, but if we are letting an outside source decide what's best for us, we are not in alignment of who we are and if we are not in alignment, our spiritual body is not fully connected to our physical body. The spiritual body has to be somewhere, so it floats somewhere around us only partly connected.

One of the things our ego likes to do is to blame and make us feel guilty. If we are doing what others have told us to do, it's easier to blame them in case something goes wrong. The fact is; it goes wrong if we are not on the same energy level as others. We talked about it earlier: what is "right" for one person might be not "right" for another.

Usually we already know deep inside if we are taking charge of our life or not. If we feel like life is happening to us instead of us making life happen we are most probably floating through life, or as the saying goes "Being swung around by the neck!"

Once we become aware of this, the next question to address is: Are we happy the way things are or would we like them to be different?

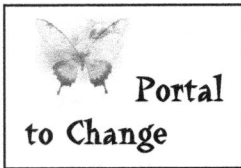

Being in Charge

Think of your life and different situations:

Write down the ones where you feel you are in charge of your situation and your actions.

Write down the ones where you feel you haven't been in charge.

Look at the situations where you feel you are in charge: What do you believe helps you to be in charge?

Do the same thing with situations where you feel you haven't been in charge. What do you believe has been stopping you from being in charge?

🦋 If you could do anything – how would you be and act in different situations (especially the ones where you feel you haven't been in charge)?

🦋 If you would be the one giving an advice to somebody in the same situation as yours, what would your advice be?

- It is important to focus on our strengths because a lack of confidence causes us to take others more seriously than ourselves. Focusing on our strengths helps us to get into an energy field where we feel good about

200

who we are which is an important part of having confidence in what we do!

The law of attraction is about the principal "like attracts like". By applying it to conscious desire: Our thoughts, (both conscious and unconscious), beliefs and emotions cause a reaction in the physical world where we "get what we think about"!

"Law of attraction" maybe a new term to us but it is not new. James Allen's book "As a Man Thinketh" which clearly explains the principle of like attracting like was published in 1902.

In 1906, William Walker Atkinson wrote "Thought Vibration or the law of attraction in the Thought World".

Writings on this subject came under various names: mental science, positive thinking, pragmatic Christianity, New Thought, Science of Mind, Religious Science.

The film and the book "The Secret" presented the "Law of Attraction". It was followed by the book "The Law of Attraction" (Esther Hicks). There might be different words used but the idea this work presents is the same – "like attract like", what you think about, comes about!

Whenever we think about wanting something in our life than we have this becomes the first step towards our goal and desired outcome. For one reason or another, we have a need for something "new" and better, and we are aware of it. This also means we have an awareness of something "old" is not working anymore. If something is not bringing us joy and happiness anymore that means something has to change. To sum it up: If we keep doing the same thing we will get the same results. If we want to have different results/outcome, we have to do something differently, we have to change.

Like Attracts Like

"Law of attraction" in other words is manifestation that all of us do as individuals and group together. Just a few basic steps to be aware of, that need to be completed in order to get what we want – to attract, to manifest it:

Know exactly what you want

Have a strong desire for what we want

Ask for what we want – either ask it to the Universe, God, Angels... or anyone else... you can ask in your mind, out loud, write it down, create the "Dream Board" (see page

Believe in what we want and believe it's possible.

Trust and have faith

Visualize ourselves already having what we want, feel it, see it, smell it, sense it...

Gratitude. Be grateful for receiving what you have already and what you want (even if it hasn't happened yet)

Believe that only good lies before you and **expect** for the best to happen.

Applying this to the topic of being different and embracing our uniqueness:

most important is to be aware and accept the idea: "yes, I am different, I am unique!" – it's **knowing** that you are unique and wanting to be just that.

Willingness to do whatever it is to get back in touch with who you are and act from place of your true self

Ask God, the Universe, Angels, Fairies – whatever you believe in – to help you to be who you are at every given moment all the time and ask them for guidance all the way through in any situation.

Believe that it is possible and safe to be who you are on the deepest level in any situation you are in

Trust that we are guided and taken care of every given moment! Have faith that no matter how challenging the journey might get – it's all for a good reason and the outcome will often be better than you might have imagined. (Because we live in such a dualistic world, to keep balanced, we often need to go through challenges before we get into a light space).

🦋 **Visualize** as clearly as we can, that we are already

🦋 **Be Grateful** for being who you are, all you have already done, all the experiences you already have had!

🦋 **Expect the best** from any situation where you are being true to yourself and expressing it, expect the best out of any situation where you are being who you are!

Dream Board

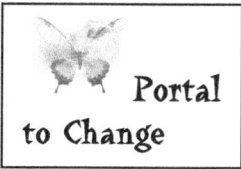

🦋 Portal
to Change

A Dream Board is a board with inspirational pictures and words that represent our dreams. It is useful and powerful tool for bringing our desires to us quicker; it plants the seeds for our dreams to come true.

Having dreams and creating a dream board is like writing down goals in life. The difference between writing goals and creating a dream board is the fact that dream board has a visual representation of our dreams, which helps our subconscious mind to focus on them without even trying. They are placed on a board where we can see them every day, thereby creating a "picture" in our mind about our dreams that serves as a request to the Universe to fulfill it!

The concept is that we attract what we think. If we put those things we want in our life right in front of us and we have a visual representation of them to look at, it makes it easier to focus on dreams and attract them into our lives.

There are many ways to make a Dream Board. However, there are certain things that are important to take into consideration when creating a dream board.

🦋 What you need for Dream board is:
A board – ideally not bendable (a bulletin board works fine), pictures of all you would like to have in your life, different color markers/ pencils/ pens, magazines with letters, picture of you, picture of symbol that presents spirituality to you, glue (or anything else that helps pictures to be where you want them to be), something to decorate the board with…

🦋 Take the board and draw a frame, ideally with gold color as gold is a color of alchemy and manifestation.

This way you give your dreams a form.

🦋 Put your picture in the middle.

🦋 Symbol of spirituality on top of it (for angel-lovers it can easily be a feather representing connection with the angelic realm…)

🦋 Then find different pictures of things you would like in your life (or something similar)… If there is anything you need to write – ideally cut out letters to form the words or words from a magazine as it allows our mind to have our desires more believable. Often we seem to underestimate ourselves, but when someone else points out our greatness, it's easier to see it for ourselves as well. It's the same with a Dream Board; if we see our desires written as if someone else would have written them, it makes them feel more real.

🦋 If any affirmations come into your mind, write them down (affirmations on the board can be written by you).

🦋 You can divide the board into several parts and focus on one topic in each part, or follow the feng-shui idea for it, with this trust your feelings.

🦋 When it comes to financial abundance – you can ask someone else to write a check for you:
Pay: your name
How much: full amount
Date: perfect Divine time
Signature: Universe

🦋 Decorating is not a "must" but you can decorate your dream board with stickers, fairy dust, push pins, glitter.

🦋 On the bottom of the board write (you can choose our own words if it feel more appropriate):
"This or something better manifests for me in perfect timing right now. Thank you!"

🦋 Ideally you are the only person that sees your dream board!

204

It's important to take time (even if it's just few minutes) every day visualizing your dreams from the dream board as if they have already come true – in detail.
Most important here is the feeling – feel as if you are living your dreams already!

Be grateful and say "thank you" to the Universe every day for fulfilling your dreams.

When we give up on our dream board (I have done that myself) and think it doesn't work, it's important to review what we have been thinking throughout the day about anything related to our dreams. For instance, if we want to create the financial freedom, but all day think negative thoughts about money, we are giving out mixed messages to the Universe. On one hand asking for abundance, on another hand, thinking about lack of abundance.

Once again it comes to taking responsibility for our actions, relying only on the Dream Board isn't enough. We can change our conscious thinking by thinking and feeling the "right" messages and intentions.

Walking our Talk

Walking our talk is to live fully from the place of "who we are", in the light of our own path.

To know who we are, to be aware of all aspects of life and ourselves is great, but it's not enough. In order to live our talk, we show who we are through actions we take. We are who we are in every situation at all times no matter how challenging it may sometimes be.

There is no other time more perfect than now to be fully here, be present, be who we are and live our true purpose.

A lot of people are not used to living their truth openly, but everything changes. The perfect time to embrace our uniqueness and live from within is now. As all great things start somewhere and start with someone, so does living our life's purpose. It can be almost addictive once our start to be our genuine self and live our truth, once we discover all the freedom and lightness it brings, it becomes easier to be our true selves.

Just like in Fairy Tales: there are lot of challenges, sometimes even "bad" seems to take over "good", but good always gets rewarded at the end and wins, so it is with living in our truth – there might be a lot of challenges, sometimes it might seem that "bad' takes over the "good", however once we stick to our truth and stay in our power, it gets rewarded abundantly!

Have Faith!

The Joy of Freedom

Being free is to be fully present, having awareness and clarity of all that there is, and living with full responsibility for our life.

Once we are our true selves at all times, there is no need to worry about what happened in the past or what will happen in future, we can enjoy NOW to the fullest.

Life's Web

Freedom is when we are in the middle of the "Life Web" where we are aware of the connection with all that there is; We connect with different people in our life, different situations, different emotions and experiences but we don't allow ourselves to over-react or to be controlled by them. We are part of all that there is, yet we are different and unique.

In our free state, we learn from our experiences, take what helps us learn or change and let go of anything else that is not needed.

When we do that our energy is clear and vibrant, which empowers our understanding and potential.

If we choose to be controlled by external influences or factors, we are giving away our personal freedom. Every thread that goes out from us and is allowed to be fed by an outside source reduces our freedom. No one else is to blame since for one reason or another we make this choice.

So the less freedom we create, the more tangled our life gets and it becomes difficult to see things for what they are.

Great affirmation for attracting freedom:

"To be free is my Divine Right and I claim it now!"

CHAPTER XII

Planting the Seeds

"What each must seek in his life never was on land or sea. It is something out of his own unique potentiality for experience, something that never has been and never could have been experienced by anyone else."
- Joseph Campbell -

Just about every living being starts as a seed. Depending on the seed, different "soil" is necessary, different care is necessary, different time for growth is necessary, different conditions, different light, and different food. What is beneficial for some seeds may be not beneficial for others.

With vegetables, we plant the seeds: we leave them and trust that one day the vegetable will grow out of the seed. But it doesn't stop there, the better care we take of the soil, the better results we get, the harvest is more abundant. We need to water the seed, give it plenty of light and anything else that it needs.

We, humans, are born from a seed as well: the joining of sex cells to form a new living thing is fertilization. In humans, a male sperm joins a female egg becoming a zygote that develops into a new organism in womb.

In plants, pollen grains containing male sex cells enter female sex cells and from this union fruit grows.

If we take care of the "soil" where the seed is planted the process of the growth and birth will be easier. In our case, the soil is the womb and it's important to look at all aspects of this "soil", physical and spiritual.

Various studies have shown that whatever the potential parents experience 2 years before becoming pregnant affects the child. What happens during the pregnancy has even more effect.

All aspects of the parent's life (especially the female), the way they feel, what they do and how, people around them, situations, food they are eating, experiences having… anything influences the baby.

Feeling safe is extremely important at this time as the baby easily adapts his parents safety level. For the Soul, being born in physical body is quite a change: being huge and enormous and squeezing in the small body. Whenever there is a change-taking place in our life, it's easy to become fearful since we don't know what changes will bring and if we look from mind-space, it can seem to be very scary not knowing what exactly will happen.

Let's look how it is in our life now - when our needs are met, when we feel comfortable, we feel supported, it helps us to move forward in our life, we feel confident about who we are and about our choices. When we feel safe to be who we are, act upon the guidance we receive and everything flows, we are happy and living a fulfilled life, having fun and enjoying all we do. It makes our heart sing, brings blessings to us and everyone else involved.

The same is happening when we are still in the womb. Our physical body is born during fertilization, our soul is being "planted" in this "new" body (like seed within a seed).

Because we are not only spiritually but also physically one with our mother while in the womb, it's impossible not to be affected by all that happens in her life. As well, it's impossible for her not to be affected by us.

If the mother is a good listener - she hears the baby's needs and allows herself to go with guidance and helps her baby and her to feel good - she fulfills the baby's needs and makes it feel safe. The more safe babies feel, the more in peace they are, the more safe are their moms since it goes both ways.

If we have been conceived in a safe space and grew in a safe environment, we would be more in tune with who we are and therefore more able to express our true and whole self – we would be in balance.

Life's Web

In the "web" idea: feeling safe and being at peace, we are in the middle. Every time some lower energy experiences happen, thread is being created to some imbalances that take away from our unique wholeness before we are even born during this lifetime (to go deeper in this direction - here we can also look on these imbalances being born in the past lifetimes and carried with us to this lifetime).

The journey continues after we are born only now we are affected by experiences and energies directly, not though our mom. If our parents are aware, they help us to remember that we are safe, we are magnificent and unique just the way we are, reminding us that it can be easy to pick up energies from other people and situations and believe them to be our

208

own, they remind us of spreading and expanding our love so only love can be attracted (throughout the years using appropriate language for certain age so that it's easy for us to understand).

If our parents are not aware, it becomes very easy to forget about these truths and become entangled. In this case more and more lower vibrating energies attach to our life, which causes us to move further and further away from the **safety of our uniqueness**.

Every time we are experiencing something new, it is like new seeds are being planted within our being. The more attention we give to them, the more we care about them – no matter if they are positive or negative, the more abundant soil we are creating for them to bloom.

Often when we become older, we are more aware of this truth and then this undoing process begins where we want to let go of all that is not needed anymore. The more energy we have given away and invested into lower energies, the more un-doing needs to be done in order to become clear again, to have clarity about any area of life. It's like weeds that we have planted in our being, even if it has happened unconsciously, it's still there. And becoming aware we also recognize what these weeds are in our life in general, in any particular situation, and we are given opportunity to pick the weeds out, replace them with wanted living beings – positive beliefs, positive affirmations, positive character...

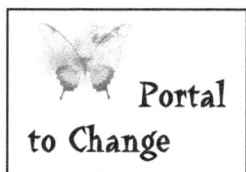

> **Portal to Change**

Meditation
Plant the Seed

Before beginning this meditation, take few deep breaths and affirm: *"I am willing to let go all the connections created that are not for my highest good. I am willing to let go of false beliefs. I am willing to embrace all things positive in my life. I ask that all the cords being created that are not for my highest good anymore, be undone in all directions and time right now. I ask that my energy field is completely cleared from any destructive energies and replaced by love and light."*

(In order for this meditation to work, you don't necessarily need to be aware of what these negative beliefs are).

One way to do this meditation is to prepare before: do an inventory of your life, different areas of life (relationships, work, family life, balance between work and play, your beliefs about yourself, your life, relationships, money, work...) and write down, what is it that you would like to have, to experience, how would you like to feel, what believes to change and to create. Then do this meditation focusing on one at the time.

Also, if you are going through some challenges in your life, you can look at the challenging situation and work on that. Make an inventory of this situation; what are your beliefs about it, what do you believe would change this situation for better, how do you feel about the situation at the present time and what would be the ideal feeling that you would like to experience in this situation.

Another way is to be spontaneous: go with a flow and allow the "right" word and energy to come in spontaneously.

Get comfortable and take few deep breaths.

Bring your attention to the 3rd eye, focus on your 3rd eye. Feel the energy swirling around and the more you focus on it, the stronger and lighter it gets: lighter energetically and lighter in color.

Visualize this energy expanding throughout your body touching every cell in your body and expanding beyond your physical body, expanding throughout your aura, your energy field. Through this light expanding, feel yourself becoming more and more connected with who you are and all that there is, feel yourself being one with who you are and all that there is.

Remember to breathe deeply and take a few minutes to be in this light.

In your mind say: " I allow myself to be connected. I allow myself to be free. I allow myself to see. I breathe in the experience. It's easy for me to see. It's easy for me to feel. It's easy for me to know exactly what I need to know at this given moment. It's easy for me to access the power within."

Now bring your attention back to the 3rd eye area.

Feel, imagine or visualize a gateway opening through your 3rd eye. See the door opening and as it happens, even more light is coming in.

Through the light you can see something forming and as it comes closer, you can see that it a pack of seeds.

If you picked some believes, emotions, affirmations to work on before the meditation, see one of them (at this time) on the package.

If you chose to be spontaneous – allow yourself to see what is written on the package.

As it comes closer see, visualize yourself opening the package and taking out seeds. Pick one of them and plant it: see it entering your body through your 3rd eye. Allow yourself to accept this new energy, new belief in you by saying in your mind: "It's safe for me to change. I allow myself to accept (name what kind of seed it is)."

See, imagine, visualize the seed entering your body and traveling through the body, touching every cell of your body from the top of your head to the tip of your toes. Then see it settling with it's glow in your inner power center (Solar Plexus chakra, Solar Plexus area – between the belly button and rib cage).

Remember to breathe deeply and allow some time for the experience.

Once the seed is in your solar plexus area, see it glowing and radiating it's energy throughout your body.

Ask the seed, what is the best care that you can give it in order for the seed and all that comes with it to grow abundantly. Allow yourself to listen as the answer can come in many different ways, like sound, vision, image, smell, idea…

The seed is planted. Remember to take good care of it so it grows abundantly within you and brings blessings to you and all involved!

If you had more than one area you wanted to work on at this time, do the meditation again choosing the other kind of seeds.

Experiment – you can also imagine that there is more than one pack of seeds at the same time and plant all the seeds one after another at once…

Abundant Blessings and
Best wishes in all you do!

AFTERWARD

My intention for this book is to encourage you to be true to yourself, accept and love yourself, "flaws" and all. That's who you are!

It's safe to be different! It's okay to be imperfect. Embrace it!

All the stories, ideas and exercises in this book were included honoring differences within each one of us and around us. My life's stories were included to show you how anything is possible and how from my deepest despair emerged the greatest gifts when I choose to embrace my uniqueness! The thought provoking ideas and exercises were included to guide you to explore your life and your own uniqueness to discover how powerful you are! Let them help you on the journey of your life!

Remember – to be your unique self is the most important job that you came here to do! You came here to express your gifts and be a joyful, magnificent being. All of us can improve our personalities, but you don't need to add or take away anything to be loved, you are loved unconditionally for being simply who you are! You are inherently loveable and unique already. You are powerful being who you are! Enjoy it and have fun in life!

The real genuine you is inside waiting for release that will bring peace, freedom and joy flowing through you.

Thank you for letting me assist you into this state of being so that your heart can sing too!

Namaste

ReGina

APPENDIX

Following are lists of websites of the mentors, therapies and places which have inspired me in my life's journey. I invite you to visit the websites listed and see what they hold for you.

❦ www.hayhouseradio.com
Best in inspirational talk radio featuring top Hay House authors.

❦ www.hayhouse.com
Publications, online news, discounts and offers, special events, product highlights, free excerpts, giveaways and more.

❦ www.louiselhay.com
❦ www.youcanhealyourlifemovie.com
Louise L. Hay – founder of the self-help movement, metaphysical lecturer and teacher and the best-selling author of numerous books, as well as the bimonthly Louise Hay Newsletter.

❦ www.angeltherapy.com
Non-denominational spiritual healing method that involves working with a person's guardian angels and archangels, to heal and harmonize every aspect of life by Doreen Virtue Ph.D, a lifelong clairvoyant who works with the angelic, elemental, and ascended-master realms.

❦ www.colourworks.org
Color Therapy System of dual colored oils and essences which powerfully translate your conscious and sub-conscious thoughts and feelings into words you can relate to, thereby releasing patterns and programming that no longer serve you.

❦ www.yoginora.com
A one-of-a-kind yoga instructor Nora Mangiamele. Her love and passion for the art of yoga shines through in every class she teaches. Her humor and eclectic music encourages everyone to strive further than they ever thought possible.

www.abraham-hicks.com
Dialogs with a group of spiritual teachers who call themselves *Abraham*.

www.colettebaronreid.com
Colette Baron-Reid is an internationally acclaimed intuitive counselor as well as a musical artist signed to the EMI Music label.

www.cloudnineyoga.com
A loving yoga "family" in Southern California led by Cloud Nine Yoga (CNY) founder *Erika Faith-Hattingh*.

www.kleine-farm-und-co.de
My favorite place in Germany where I first experienced being accepted for who I am. Horses and other animals, energy work, birthday parties for children, holiday apartments and a lot of fun.

www.deniselinn.com
Denise Linn internationally respected healer, writer, and teacher. An expert in feng shui and space clearing, soul coaching and past lives.

www.thegongmaster.org
The Gong Master *Sotantar Salvador*. Gong Baths and meditation, healing concerts to celebrate the peace, love and joy.

www.commonground191.com
Commonground191 an amazing project by *Gary Simpson*. His vision involves creating "a large series of abstract panels one for each country.

www.sacredspaceswa.com & www.angelichuman.com
Toni Elizabeth Sar'h Petrinovich, Ph.D. communicates with Orbs of Light.

www.sharonrenae.com
I received my very first angel reading.

ONLINE RESOURCES

About Latvia

www.state.gov

www.li.lv

www.latviansonline.com

www.sciforums.com

www.haldjas.folklore.ee

www.cunina.com

www.dictionary.reference.com

Indigo Resources

www.starchild.co.za

www.namastecafe.com

www.indigosociety.com

www.indigoevolution.com

www.childrenofthenewearth.com

www.starlite.com

www.indigochild.com

www.indigochild.net

BIBLIOGRAPHY

Allen, James. *As a Man Thinketh.* Cornerstone Books, 1902

Byrne, Rhonda, Paul Harrington, Rev. Dr. Michael Beckwith, and Neale Donald Walsch. *The Secret DVD.* TS Production LLC, 2006

Caroll, Lee & Tober, Jan. *Indigo Children: The New Kids Have Arrived.* Hay House, 1999

Cooper, Diana. *The Golden Years of Atlantis Meditation.* 2005

Emoto, Masaru. *The True Power of Water: Healing and Discovering Ourselves.* Simon & Schuster, 2005

Farmer, Steven D. Ph.D. *Animal Spirit Guides.* Hay House, 2006

Hay, Louise L. *You Can Heal Your Life-The Movie*: Expanded Version DVD. Hay House, 2007

Hicks, Esther and Jerry. *The Law of Attraction; The Basics of the Teachings of the Abraham.* Hay House, 2006

Losey, Meg Blackburn Msc.D. Ph.D. *Children of Now.* Career Press, 2007

Losey, Meg Blackburn Msc.D. Ph.D. *Conversation with Children of Now.* Career Press, 2008

Virtue, Doreen Ph.D. *Angel Guidance Board.* Hay House, 2005

Virtue, Doreen Ph.D. *Crystal Children.* Hay House, 2003

Virtue, Doreen Ph.D. *Earth Angels.* Hay House, 2002

Virtue, Doreen Ph.D. *Healing with the Angels Oracle Cards.* Hay House, 1999

Virtue, Doreen Ph.D. *Realms of the Earth Angels.* Hay House, 2007

Virtue, Doreen Ph.D. *The Care and Feeding of Indigo Children.* Hay House, 2001

Kestners Ēriks. *Emīls, divas Lotiņas un citi.* Liesma, 1983.

Preußler, Otfried. *Die Kleine Hexe.* Thienemann Verlag, 1997

Terhef, Rena. *Tarot für Zauberhexen.* Königfurt Urania, 2001

ABOUT THE AUTHOR

In every area of her life, author ReGina Norlinde, has always felt very different from everyone around her. She is one of the children of a higher degree of evolution than "normal" that are called **Indigo Children**: highly spiritual, extremely sensitive, wise beyond their years...

ReGina Norlinde was born in Latvia. After graduating the University at the age of 22, she left her home country to travel and live abroad. Feeling different has created ReGina's life's journey to be full of challenges that have led her to understanding of universal truth and revelations of her own special gifts which brought about self-acceptance, personal freedom and blessings beyond her imagination.

Scotland was the place where ReGina fully claimed her uniqueness at the age of 28 and ever since then, she has been in service of helping others around the world on their life's journey using the tools she has gathered from her experience.

ReGina is an International Speaker and Spiritual Teacher, Intuitive Counselor, ANGEL THERAPIST®, Medium and Color Therapist. She currently resides in California, USA.

More information on ReGina and her services can be found at www.stardusthealing.com

Her weekly radio show you can find on www.earthangelradio.com

Latvian Folklore Photo by Mārīte Meļķe

Mārīte Meļķe is a program director for a recreation center in Valka, Latvia.

She has also been the director of the folk group "Nāburgi" since it first started on February 10th, 1990.

The folk group "Nāburgi' performs folk songs and games from different regions of Latvia. The musical instruments that members of this group play are the accordion, kokle (Latvian national instrument), violin, zither, drums and different smaller instruments. Every three years they take part in an international folk festival called "Baltica" and have performed in singing and dancing festivals since 1990. The next "Baltica" will be held in July 2009.

"Nāburgi" performs in other countries including Israel, Italy, Germany, Estonia, Sweden, Belgium, Poland and Lithuana. The oldest member of this group is 62 years old, the youngest is 10 years old.

("Nāburgi")

*"My wish for each one of you is: **be who you are, do what makes your heart sing and shine your light brightly into the world because it is the most important job that you are here to do!**"*

- ReGina Norlinde -

www.ingramcontent.com/pod-product-compliance
Lightning Source LLC
Chambersburg PA
CBHW031249090426
42742CB00007B/384